Women's Health and Human Rights

The Promotion and Protection of Women's Health through International Human Rights Law

Rebecca J. Cook
Associate Professor (Research) and
Director, International Human Rights Programme
Faculty of Law, University of Toronto
Toronto, Canada

World Health Organization
Geneva
1994

W9-CYG-674

WHO Library Cataloguing in Publication Data

Women's health and human rights : the promotion and protection of women's health through international
  human rights law.
  1.Women's health 2.Human rights — legislation
  ISBN 92 4 156166 1   (NLM Classification: WA 300)

PRINTED IN SWITZERLAND
94/9961 — Strategic — 7 500

Contents

Foreword

This publication was originally prepared as a contribution by the World Health Organization to the World Conference on Human Rights in 1993. As such it approaches the subject of women's health from the perspective of international human rights law.

This is a lawyer's view of women's health, and not the view of a health specialist or a patient or politician. Dr Rebecca Cook, a specialist in human rights law, has examined the international human rights treaties that States have signed and the implications those treaties have for action to improve women's health.

Many societies attribute low status to women and the social roles they are required to perform. This "devaluation" of women often leads to a denial of rights — such as the right to access to information, adequate nutrition and health services such as family planning — to which they are entitled by the very fact that their governments have signed international agreements. Some 500 000 women die each year from preventable causes related to complications of pregnancy and childbirth. Yet many societies, giving low status to women, accept maternal death as the natural order of things.

In terms of modern human rights law, which guarantees equity between the sexes, many of the health disadvantages of women can be classified as injustices. Maternal death, for example, is only the end point in a series of injustices that many women face. They eat last and eat least, are undereducated and overworked. They are recognized for their childbearing capacity with little attention paid to anything else they can do.

Women's rights in the health care sector may be violated by the lack of certain health services. They may be violated by lack of information about their health options, or simply a lack of appropriate technology to ease their burden inside and outside the home. Today, the ranks of the poor are disproportionately filled with single women who are heads of households. These poor women, as well as young girls, resort to coping strategies which include recourse to low-paid jobs in environments fraught with known risks to their own health, and to that of future generations. Many of them are easy prey to the rising number of prostitution rings, and are victims of violence — rape and other physical abuse — which is accentuated in periods of crisis such as ethnic conflict and war. When judging state compliance with human rights instruments relating to health, it is essential that the health of women be seriously considered.

Health legislation has contributed substantially to promoting public health and could be used more vigorously to promote women's health. The international community should be motivated by existing positive examples of legislation that has enhanced the health of women.

In spite of ill-health in women, often linked with socioeconomic conditions, women are survivors. Throughout history, they have survived war, famine, drought and disease, and have ensured the survival of their children, their families and their communities. They should be encouraged and supported to take advantage of the many basic human rights and freedoms that empower them to realize their own health goals.

A dynamic feature of the human rights framework is the possibility of using it in a proactive way in which a culture of equal worth and dignity of all human beings is fostered and the principle of non-discrimination, whether this concerns access to existing goods and services or allowing for participation and freedom of choice, is respected.

The women of the world need more than treaties. They need urgent action to make the terms of these instruments a reality in their lives and in their access to health. This publication is a guide to how that action can be achieved.

Dr A El Bindari Hammad

Acknowledgements

This publication was prepared in the context of the Global Commission on Women's Health for the World Conference on Human Rights, June 1993.

Contributors included: Ms J.P. Alexander, Mrs M.-J. Bernardi, Dr D. Blake, Miss K.L. Bond, Mr D. Bramley, Mrs J. Cottingham, Mr S.S. Fluss, Ms M. Haslegrave, Dr M.J. Hirschfeld, Dr M. Law, Dr J. Leslie, Dr S. Lyagoubi-Ouahchi, Mrs C.A. Mulholland, Miss G. Pinet, Mr L. Porter, Dr J. Rochon, Dr M. Simpson-Hebert, Ms J. Spicehandler, Mr M.A. Subramanian, Dr R. Thapa, Dr T. Türmen, Dr C.K. Vlassoff, Mrs A.S. Williams and Mrs S. Zolfaghari, under the general coordination of Dr A. El Bindari Hammad.

The World Health Organization would like to acknowledge the generous contribution received from the Carnegie Corporation of New York which has made this publication possible.

The World Health Organization is also grateful to the following for providing source material: Dr U. Amazigo, University of Nigeria, Nsukka; Dr L. Brabin, Liverpool School of Tropical Medicine; Dr M. Buvinic, International Centre for Research on Women, Washington, DC; Mrs J. Hausermann, Rights and Humanity, London; Dr M. Koblinsky, Mothercare/John Snow Inc., Arlington, VA; Ms B. Ras-Work, Inter-African Committee, Addis Ababa; Dr L. Heise, Rutgers University, New Brunswick, NJ; Dr C. Meslem, United Nations Office at Vienna; UNICEF; and others too numerous to mention.

CHAPTER 1
The evolution of international human rights relevant to women's health

The understanding of "health" in international legal practice is conditioned by the definition of health employed in the Constitution of the World Health Organization (WHO) (1), which was signed on 22 July 1946 and entered into force on 7 April 1948:

> Health is a state of complete physical, mental and social well-being and not merely the absence of disease or infirmity.

The legal implication of a broad concept of health is that States have duties both to promote health, social, and related services, and to prevent or remove barriers to the realization and maintenance of women's physical, mental, and social well-being. The challenge of securing women's health directs attention not simply to physical and mental health services, but to the justice of the foundations upon which societies function.

The modern era of rights that can be applied to women's health may be said to have commenced with the adoption of the United Nations Charter in 1945. Earlier international instruments addressed the rights of women but did so from a predominantly paternalistic perspective that protected women from such risks as night-time employment. The Charter (2) opens with the provision that the purposes of the United Nations include:

> to achieve international co-operation in solving international problems of an economic, social, cultural, or humanitarian character, and in promoting and encouraging respect for human rights and for fundamental freedoms for all without distinction as to ... sex ...

This Charter requires the United Nations to promote "higher standards of living ... and conditions of economic and social progress and development" and "solutions of international economic, social, health, and related problems". In order to encourage "respect for the principle of equal rights ...", the United Nations is to promote "universal respect for, and observance of, human rights and fundamental freedoms for all without distinction as to ... sex ..."(2).

The United Nations Charter prepared the ground for further universal and regional international instruments. In 1948, the Universal Declaration of Human Rights (3) was adopted by the United Nations General Assembly. This Declaration was emphatic in condemning discrimination on grounds of sex, and set forth a network of rights relevant to the promotion and protection of health. The Declaration was developed into international human rights law by two general Covenants, both adopted by the General Assembly in 1966, namely the International Covenant on Civil and Political Rights (the Political Covenant) (4) and the International Covenant on Economic, Social and Cultural Rights (the Economic Covenant) (5).

Similarly derived from the Universal Declaration are regional human rights conventions, including the European Convention for the Protection of Human Rights and Fundamental Freedoms (the European Convention) (6) and its Social Charter (7), the American Convention on Human Rights (the American Convention) (8) and its Additional Protocol in the Area of Economic, Social and Cultural Rights, and the African Charter on Human and Peoples' Rights (the African Charter) (9). These regional conventions all prohibit discrimination on grounds of sex and require respect for various rights related to the promotion and protection of health.

Other specialized conventions relevant to women's health exist, such as the International Convention on the Elimination of All Forms of Racial Discrimination (the Race Convention) (10), which prevents discrimination against women of racial groups, the Convention on the Rights of the Child (the Children's Convention) (11), which protects the rights of girl children, the Convention against Torture and Other Cruel, Inhuman or Degrading Treatment or Punishment (12), which prohibits the infliction of physical or mental pain or suffering on women, and the Convention relating to the Status of Refugees (13), which provides protection for refugee women.

The leading modern instrument on women's equal rights, derived from the Universal Declaration, is the Convention on the Elimination of All Forms of Discrimination against Women (the Women's Convention) (14), adopted in 1979. The Women's Convention is the definitive international legal instrument requiring respect for and observance of the human rights of women. This Convention is universal in reach and comprehensive in scope. The Convention is the first international treaty in which Member countries, known as States Parties, assume the legal duty to eliminate all forms of discrimination against women in civil, political, economic, social and cultural areas, including health care and family planning. As of 1 January 1994, 130 countries had become States Parties to this Convention (see Annex 1).

This wide acceptance of the Women's Convention demonstrates both the strength and the weakness of international human rights law. The weakness is that treaties obtain their legally binding character only when States voluntarily become members of them, usually by ratification. The strength is that States can feel morally obliged and politically advantaged to show their membership of human rights treaties, and they therefore accept the price that membership imposes of complying with the obligations that make rights effective.

The Women's Convention obliges States Parties in general "to pursue by all appropriate means and without delay a policy of eliminating discrimination against women", and in particular "to eliminate discrimination against women in the field of health care in order to ensure ... access to health care services, including those related to family planning" (14). States Parties thereby assume obligations reliably to determine risks to women's health. The means chosen by States Parties to attack dangers to health will be determined by national considerations, such as women's access to appropriate health care, patterns of health service delivery and the epidemiology of women's morbidity and mortality. The emerging international imperative is that the means chosen by States should lead to the promotion and protection of women's health and should enhance the dignity of women and their capacity for self-determination.

Rights to the removal of laws, practices, stereotypes and prejudices that impair women's well-being are rights that are relevant to women's health. Rights to access to health through education and health services are also necessary. When women experience disadvantage in contrast to other members of their families, communities or societies, they will be considered to suffer discrimination because they are women. When their families, communities or societies are disadvantaged in contrast to other families, communities or societies, women suffer compounded disadvantages related to such features as race, class and, for instance, geographical location.

Human rights treaties, by their terms, establish committees to monitor compliance with the treaties. For example, the Committee on the Elimination of Discrimination against Women (CEDAW) is the treaty body established to monitor compliance with the Women's Convention. Other treaty-based bodies, such as the Human Rights Committee and the Committee on Economic, Social and Cultural Rights, are established to monitor compliance with the Political Covenant and the Economic Covenant respectively. All major human rights treaties provide for a system of reporting to the treaty bodies.

States Parties are required to make regular reports on the steps taken to implement their obligations and the difficulties they have experienced in doing so. Reports are examined by the relevant treaty bodies in the presence of representatives of the reporting States. Some of the treaty bodies, such as the Human Rights Committee, also have the authority to receive petitions from individuals claiming violations of the treaty by their governments.

The WHO understanding of health transcends the elimination of disease and infirmity, and addresses physical, mental and social well-being. Accordingly, attention must be given to the full range of human rights that go beyond the provision of medical, nursing and related health services, and that contribute in different ways and at different levels to the achievement and maintenance of health as defined by WHO. Therefore, rights relevant to the promotion and protection of women's health include:

- the right of women to be free from all forms of discrimination;
- rights relating to individual freedom and autonomy, including rights regarding survival, liberty and security, rights regarding family and private life, and rights to information and education;
- rights to health care and the benefits of scientific progress;
- rights regarding women's empowerment, including the rights to freedom of thought and assembly and the right to political participation.

The purposes of this publication are to examine the relevance of these international human rights to the promotion and protection of women's health (see Annex 2), and to provide a framework for future analysis and for cross-fertilization and collaboration among organizations concerned with human rights and women's health in order that:

- the scope and content of human rights can be further elaborated for the more effective promotion and protection of women's health;
- the nature of State obligations to implement human rights with regard to women's health can be further articulated and publicized.

Finally, this publication seeks to explain the mechanisms at international, regional and national levels that are available for holding states accountable for compliance with their human rights treaty obligations with regard to the promotion and protection of women's health.

CHAPTER 2
Pervasive neglect of women's health

Overview

T he familiar WHO concept that health is determined by reference to "physical, mental and social well-being and not merely the absence of disease or infirmity" emphasizes the significance of the social welfare of populations and not merely the medicalization of disease. Medical science occupies a central position in health, but health is the outcome of a combination of factors — biological, genetic, environmental and socio-economic. The elements that condition a population's health go beyond physiological factors to include gross national product, wealth distribution and access to income-earning capacity and opportunities, availability of and access to educational resources, the urban and rural living environment and physical infrastructure, and, for instance, political structures through which individuals and groups can influence distribution of resources that affect health status (15). Circumstances affecting health can accordingly be analysed through various statistical indicators of social and economic functioning and at different levels of abstraction, from the individual, the family, the community or group whose members identify with each other, to higher levels of social definition culminating in the nation itself.

In some regions of the world, women are seen as relatively insignificant. At the individual level, women are often conditioned to suffer low self-esteem, to accept an inferior status as natural and to find in the birth of daughters a source of failure, apology and distress (16). Families identify themselves through names often derived from and continued by the male line. Legal, religious and cultural doctrines may reinforce the devaluation of daughters. Devaluation of women of all ages moves beyond matters of status and spiritual concerns into the area of material interests when daughters cost dowry payments so that they may marry into other families. Money spent on education earns no return for the family when women leave the family on marriage, are unemployable when unmarried, or become outcasts through pregnancy before marriage. Daughters-in-law warrant no investment when they may die through pregnancy, become infertile or suffer infections or disgrace that lead to divorce or abandonment by their husbands. The cumulative impact of women's multifaceted disadvantages and their devaluation within legal, religious and cultural traditions and socioeconomic systems result in many women being denied health as understood by WHO. Their disadvantages spiral downwards, in that their liability to death in pregnancy or to infertility contributes to their devaluation, while their devaluation contributes to poor health and greater liability to illness and premature death (17).

Neglect of women's health is pervasive, on grounds of both their sex and their gender. *Sex* is determined by genes and biology, whereas *gender* may be understood as a social construct that addresses "personality traits, attitudes, feelings, values, behaviours and activities that society ascribes to the two sexes on a differential basis" (18). Women suffer discrimination in health and other matters because of their sex, as for instance in cases of taboos and dysfunctions related to menstruation (19, 20). Women suffer additional discrimination, however, because roles identified with female gender are not valued in social and economic terms. Those who perform domestic and child care work in their own homes are frequently regarded as "unemployed" and ineligible for non-monetary benefits related to paid employment, such as occupational health and safety protection. Roles ascribed to men — traditionally hunters, warriors or bread-winners — carry higher prestige than the role of home-maker and afford priority in entitlement to the rewards of family effort.

Service roles associated with females — particularly in nursing, auxiliary health care and child care — have almost invariably been low-paid. "Feminine" roles carry less significance and credibility than those associated with masculinity, and are less valued and protected. Neglect of women's health in pregnancy and childbirth may be rationalized by acceptance of the natural order or divine will that destines women to liability to death in childbearing (21). Segments of society that suffer most health disadvantages — such as low-income groups and the elderly — often tend to have a predominance of women.

A modern understanding has emerged that is sensitive to the disadvantages experienced by women, in both developing and developed countries, in pursuing health as understood by WHO. Studies demonstrate causes of disadvantage at different levels of analysis, and modern law on internationally protected human rights classifies many of these disadvantages as injustices. For instance, maternal mortality can be explained through the immediate cause of lack of maternity care, through the underlying causes of exhaustion and anaemia associated with multiparity and short intervals between births, and through structural causes such as poverty.

Human rights law addresses state responsibility for immediate denial or obstruction of obstetric services through the right to health care. The right to education, among other rights, addresses the underlying cause of multiparity. Women and men who can read about and understand the health benefits to women, newborn children and previously born children of a minimum spacing of two years between pregnancies would recognize incentives for birth spacing. States may be considered legally responsible for the structural cause of poverty when they allocate available national wealth disproportionately to expenditures such as military armaments that deny their populations their basic needs (22). The international legal order may also address national poverty through the claimed right to development (23).

The immediate, underlying and structural causes of morbidity and mortality can vary from country to country, from disease to disease and among socioeconomic classes and ethnic populations (24). A variation of major significance within populations, however, is the difference between men and women that research and practice have failed adequately to identify. Apart from addressing obvious differences in reproductive function, research on populations has tended to be undifferentiated by sex and has excluded proper studies of women. Exclusion of women from much clinical and physiological research has been explained on the grounds that the menstrual cycle introduces a potentially confounding variable in analysis of data that can be overcome only by larger subject pools and more complex data gathering and analysis. A protective reason has been that experimental use of products and therapies might expose fetuses to unknown risk, and excluding women subjects who might be pregnant involves indelicate or intrusive questioning or testing (25).

The fact that women are physiologically distinguishable from men in far more ways than reproductive function and hormonal status reduces the relevance to women of research and health interventions based on male or undifferentiated populations (26). Women have different body shape, organ size and volume, and distribution of body fat, so that for instance the bioavailability of therapeutic drugs differs between the sexes.

As a result, health problems need to be analysed from the perspective of women because they suffer from:

- diseases or conditions that affect men and women differently;
- diseases or conditions unique to women or some groups of women;
- diseases or conditions that are more prevalent in women;
- diseases or conditions that are more serious among women or among some groups of women;
- diseases or conditions for which the risk factors are different for women or for some groups of women;
- diseases or conditions for which the interventions are different for women or for some groups of women.

There is a real need at national, regional and international levels to improve the prevention, diagnosis and treatment of illnesses in women and to extend research on diseases and conditions that affect women.

Risk factors for poor health can be analysed by reference to a wide variety of criteria, and women at risk can be classified by such features as age, socioeconomic status, literacy and educational status, family structure and ethnic grouping. A number of features that condition adverse health consequences for women at different points in their life cycle are identified below. This list of features, which is neither exhaustive nor comprehensive, sets the context within which human rights law may be invoked to provide relief, remedy and preferably preventive interventions.

Health risks in infancy and childhood

At birth, female newborns may be a disappointment to their parents because of their sex. Indeed, evidence indicates that couples in some countries have resorted to prenatal diagnosis of fetal sex for the purpose only of aborting female fetuses. Newborn females not subject to infanticide may suffer neglect of nursing and feeding, and may succumb to malnutrition (18). There is evidence that girls are born with a biological advantage over boys and are innately more resistant to infection and malnutrition, but this advantage is often cancelled by social disadvantages (27). Surviving daughters suffer the health ravages of malnutrition where they are disfavoured by family feeding sequences set by their mothers. Discrimination in nutrition is not limited to social classes that suffer scarcity of resources (18).

Girl children are disadvantaged in education when parents neglect to send them to school, as in cases when they are required to care for younger children and to assist mothers in such domestic chores as carrying water, gathering fuel wood and preparing food. Denied literacy, such girls gain no independent exposure either to education that can reveal alternative choices for their future or to knowledge of preventive health care such as hygiene.

A particular risk that girls suffer in certain regions of the world is female circumcision, conditioned by a variety of perceptions and values within families and societies that engage in this practice (28). Usually undertaken before menarche, and often at eight or nine years of age, the procedure is a direct cause of many ailments and an indirect cause of many more. Physical health consequences vary according to the severity of the method of circumcision used. The health consequences of infibulation, the severest form, include infection, tetanus, shock, haemorrhage, septicaemia and urine retention. Longer-term physical complications in-

8

clude urinary and reproductive tract infections which may result in infertility, menstrual disorders, vesicovaginal fistulae, and difficulties during childbirth, including obstructed labour that can compromise the safety and very survival of mothers and children (29). WHO estimates that 80–100 million women in sub-Saharan Africa have been subjected to circumcision, of whom 15 million have been infibulated. This figure excludes estimates from south-east Asia and immigrant communities in developed countries where the problem is also known to exist.

Health risks of adolescence

Beyond the cumulative health effects young females suffer as a result of disadvantaged childhood, they face additional risks in adolescence. Their emerging sexuality offers a promise for their future but is also a source of vulnerability if they are not free to decide when to make themselves sexually available and to whom. Early pregnancy is a risk that may be aggravated by disgrace and ostracism if it occurs before marriage. Maternal mortality rates are highest among teenage mothers, and risk is compounded by liability to repeated early pregnancy. Sexual abuse and family and economic pressures to engage in prostitution present adverse environments for adolescent health, including exposure to sexually transmitted diseases. The risk of infection with the human immunodeficiency virus (HIV) is attracting many men to increasingly younger sexual partners. In many settings, sexual exploitation may predispose adolescents to abuse of illicit drugs. In both developed and developing countries, adolescent females may be specially targeted by advertisers of tobacco and alcohol products, further predisposing them to the immediate and long-term health consequences of dependence.

Marriage or pregnancy may disqualify an adolescent girl from continued schooling and the responsibilities of nursing and child care may in any case prevent her attendance, resulting in the health consequences of poor education and limited opportunities for employment and income-earning. Work in the home, frequently that of a young woman's in-laws, will include caring for elderly and sick relatives and the physical burdens of attending to the animals and agriculture.

Health risks of women at work

Work performed in the home, frequently misrepresented as "unemployment", presents no fewer hazards to health than industrial employment. Work in the home may require malnourished women to toil for long hours in carrying heavy burdens, in preparing food over stoves heated by smoke-generating fuels in unventilated spaces, and in domestic agriculture. Exposure to heating fuels and household chemicals will often be significantly greater among women than among men. Injuries from accidents in the home, including burning and scalding, are often as frequent as injuries in the workplace. Skeletal damage from carrying heavy weights, including fetching water, is more common among women than among men in certain parts of the world (30).

Women competing for employment with men may be at greater risk of harm from heavy toil and physical hazards, and women in employment that is typically "feminine" are liable to suffer low pay and long hours. Women in employment outside the home frequently bear a double burden in that, after earning a hard day's pay, they are responsible for all the domestic work in their homes. This aggravates the health strains that affect them and limits time for self-care and recuperation.

Reproductive health

An explanation of reproductive health that reflects the WHO concept of health (31) is that it is:

> a condition in which the reproductive process is accomplished in a state of complete physical, mental and social well-being and is not merely the absence of disease or disorders of the reproductive process. Reproductive health, therefore, implies that people have the ability to reproduce, to regulate their fertility and to practise and enjoy sexual relationships. It further implies that reproduction is carried to a successful outcome through infant and child survival, growth and healthy development. It finally implies that women can go safely through pregnancy and childbirth, that fertility regulation can be achieved without health hazards and that people are safe in having sex.

Epidemiological and comparable data show how lack of basic obstetric services, prenatal care and related reproductive health services result in unnecessarily high rates of maternal mortality and morbidity (32, 33). WHO has estimated that each year 500 000 women die from pregnancy-related causes and that in different countries unsafe abortion can cause "25 to 50 percent of [maternal] deaths, simply because women do not have access to family planning services they want and need, or have no access to safe procedures or to humane treatment for the complications of abortion" (34).

Evidence also confirms the danger to health presented by pregnancies that come too early, too late, too often and at intervals that are too closely spaced in women's reproductive lives (35). Unskilled abortion procedures can endanger life, health and future fertility. Unwanted infertility, itself often a consequence of infection resulting from poor health care, leads to unmarriageability, divorce or abandonment and the health disadvantages associated with them, particularly where women's independent economic capacities are limited by gender discrimination in employment.

Fear of sexual relationships leading to unwanted pregnancy, often related to the physical dangers of pregnancy, impairs women's enjoyment of health as defined by WHO. Social and religious pressure may make women ambivalent about their sexual instincts, in contrast to men whose aggressive virility is often presented and perceived as a positive attribute. In contrast to men, women who are sexually active before or outside marriage are often devalued as immoral people and often stereotyped as promiscuous sources of infection of men.

Although monitors of the acquired immunodeficiency syndrome (AIDS) and HIV infection were slow to recognize the impact of the virus on women's health, concern with AIDS and HIV infection has recycled the image of women "not as individuals, but merely as vectors of virus transmission" (36).

Only recently has attention been given to the small amount of information available from clinical studies on HIV infection regarding the effects of disease processes or medical interventions on women. It has been observed (37) that:

> the original interest in HIV-infected women centered on their relation to paediatric AIDS through perinatal transmission. A search of the medical literature yields only a handful of papers focusing on the consequences of the infection in nonpregnant women.

Women may be disadvantaged in protecting themselves against HIV infection not only through lack of information but also through lack of power to deny partners intercourse, to insist that partners use condoms or to obtain supplies of the new female condom (38). Where health professionals are reluctant to provide services to HIV-infected patients, women who are HIV-positive or who are suspected to be HIV-positive may find that gynaecological examinations, prenatal care, abortions and services in childbirth become unavailable to them, perhaps because of the status or lifestyle of their partners. Health professionals have been seen to react judgementally to patients who engage in high-risk behaviour for HIV infection, without being subject to discipline for professional misconduct or violation of their employing institutions' by-laws or regulations (39, 40).

Violence against women

Physical and psychological injuries caused by violence against women, including assaults by husbands, have been inadequately recognized, diagnosed and treated, in part because of the social stigma attached to the causes of such injuries. In some communities, however, physical force is not considered a wrongful act and assaultive men attract no stigma or condemnation. In industrialized countries, assaults have been reported to cause more injuries to women than motor vehicle accidents, rape and muggings combined (*41*). An added dimension concerns abuse of the elderly since a high proportion of the elderly are women.

Failure to identify injuries to women as deliberately inflicted by their partners or guardians parallels medical failure to identify injuries to children as being due to child abuse committed by adult guardians. From insensitive clumsiness, through exploitation to physical violence, women experience both inside and outside their homes assaults on their integrity and bodies that deny them the sense of well-being, security and esteem that contributes to health.

Other health problems of increasing concern

Because of women's lower social status, the impact of many other diseases on women has been largely ignored. This is true in the case of diseases such as malaria, leprosy, onchocerciasis, lymphatic filariasis, leishmaniasis, schistosomiasis and tuberculosis. Recent studies show that, while they may not be infected more than men by these diseases, women tend to suffer more severe consequences (*42*). This is often a result of the stigma attached to such diseases, the fact that women often deny their symptoms until they are too severe to ignore and their feelings of guilt as illness prevents them fulfilling their expected care-giving role in the household.

Until recently, gender differences in diseases such as cancer and heart disease, the two major killers of women in industrialized countries, were also largely ignored, as was the differential effect of drugs for treatment of these diseases on men and women (*43*). Men have invariably been taken as the standard for clinical tests, and it is only now that the inadequacy of this standard when applied to women is becoming recognized.

Problems of the elderly, particularly in industrialized countries, are also increasingly important. Although women live longer than men on average, little attention has been paid to gender differences in the quality of life among the elderly or to the illnesses from which they may suffer. It is known that one consequence of women's longer life span is a longer period of overall morbidity.

CHAPTER 3
Measuring state compliance with treaty obligations

W hen a State is bound by an international human rights treaty to observe a particular right, the question arises of legal definition of what respect for that right requires. A related question is how compliance with the human right is determined and, in particular, how breach of the right is established. The purpose of Chapter 3 is to provide a framework for these questions to be addressed in the context of women's health. In order for these questions to be answered there should be cross-fertilization and collaboration among organizations concerned with human rights and women's health. There is a particular need for collaboration between organizations that have been working on criteria to measure State compliance with human rights treaties and those that have been working on statistical indicators for women's health.

Specialized agencies that develop statistical indicators of performance serve a vital role in permitting States to demonstrate their compliance with standards of observance of international human rights (44, 45, 46). Promising advances have been made by human rights bodies towards the development and refinement of criteria relevant to human rights in general (47) and to economic, social and cultural rights in particular (48, 49, 50). In this respect, WHO's existing indicators and criteria regarding women's health are useful and offer an opportunity for fuller utilization by the relevant bodies.

What are we trying to measure?

In using the indicators mentioned above, the Recommendations of the Seminar on Appropriate Indicators to Measure Achievements in the Progressive Realization of Economic, Social and Cultural Rights suggest that further work is necessary to:

- clarify the nature, scope and contents of the specific rights enumerated in the [Economic] Covenant;
- define more precisely those aspects of the individual rights that are of immediate application, including the core content of the rights and of minimum standards of achievement;

- identify the minimum steps to be taken by States Parties in order that they might comply with their legal obligations to take steps towards the progressive realization of the rights, in the Limburg Principles on the implementation of the International Covenant on Economic, Social and Cultural Rights, the General Comments of the Committee on Economic, Social and Cultural Rights and the developments at other international human rights fora (51).

Taking the above into consideration, it would be necessary first to identify and clarify the core content of the rights and obligations that relate to the promotion and protection of women's health. The qualitative and quantitative indicators which will assist in measuring State compliance with those obligations should then be determined.

WHO has given guidance on determining compliance with international human rights affecting health in its Global Indicators for Monitoring and Evaluating Health for All by the Year 2000 (52). Indicators may centre on health status, for example the infant mortality rate of a population. Other indicators may relate to health service coverage, showing for example the extent of primary health care. Such indicators may reveal over time whether a particular country is meeting its legal obligation of progressive development towards full protection of the right to health care.

Indicators are neutral instruments of assessment when they are established by reference to criteria relevant to the health and vital statistics information that most countries gather. Indicators may furnish countries with shields against criticism for failing to meet legal duties of care for women's health and may furnish critics with weapons that open State practice to scrutiny. Indicators may equip States to discharge their reporting responsibilities under international human rights treaties such as the Women's Convention. They also permit scrutinizing committees acting under authority of such conventions to describe the information they require and serve advance notice of the obligations with which they will monitor compliance.

Statistics on health coverage and health status have limits, however, because they will generally indicate only a national average and tend not to be disaggregated by sex or, for example, by income level. Statistics will not necessarily indicate, for instance, the lack of health services for women in rural villages. In such a situation, women's rights to health care might be violated because of lack of certain health services, and data disaggregated by region might help indicate whether such violations have occurred. Furthermore, data on health status will not necessarily indicate whether women are adequately informed about their health options so that they can decide on particular courses of treatment. In this case, rights to liberty might be violated and data on specific events might help indicate whether such violations have occurred. In neither situation will the indicators show the cause of the violations or whether legal responsibility can be attributed to the State. Both causes of violations and their attribution to the State are usually needed to establish the legal responsibility of the State.

The kinds of indicators that are needed will vary according to the context of women's experiences and to the rights in question. Efforts in this direction should be considered as part of research or periodic evaluation of programmes and services and not as an added burden on the health service information system. It should be noted that in the recommendations for monitoring progress towards the health goals of the World Summit for Children, WHO and UNICEF encourage that the indicators be disaggregated by sex and setting.

The core content of rights relating to the promotion and protection of women's health has to be informed by women and their needs with regard to their own health. In legal analysis, a method to determine women's needs must be developed (53). This is all the more important since most laws have been enacted by men and it is now realized that these laws do not always take effects on women into account. In addressing women's needs, consideration must be given not only to the consequences of laws, but also to the consequences of, for instance, health care delivery systems, medical research and allocations of health care resources.

The use of empirical evidence and legal methods that are sensitive to women's needs provides insight into the law's neglect of women's health and may expose long-held beliefs in the neutrality of laws that in fact disadvantage women in the most fundamental ways.

Empirical surveys and epidemiological studies, including those developed by the United Nations and its specialized agencies (32), show how neglect of women's health results in avoidably high levels of maternal and infant death and sickness, and leads to exclusion of women from educational, economic and social opportunities.

The challenge is to ensure that women's perspectives are included in legal, ethical and related analysis of the circumstances of women's lives in order to lift women's invisibility and better understand and remedy injustice. This approach to law can also be applied to medical information and the organization of health care systems. It can be used by those who have a thorough understanding of women's health at differing individual, community and national levels. Indicators properly attuned to women's environments and health circumstances can first demonstrate injustice and then serve as instruments for measuring reform.

What is the scope and content of the right?

The scope and the content of the human right are specific to each right in question and to the overall object and purpose of the human rights treaty that embodies the particular right. For example, the scope of a right may be non-discrimination on grounds of sex, which requires that women be treated equally with men and have equal access with men to a public good. In contrast to non-discrimination rights, the right may protect individual security as such. The protection of individual security does not depend on whether others enjoy that same security but whether in a particular situation a woman's security was denied.

In addition to non-discrimination rights and individual rights, there are human rights that enable individuals to participate in civic and public affairs, such as the right to assembly, and rights that provide a basic need for living, such as health care. The scope and content of these rights evolve according to the circumstances of the times. If these rights are going to be applied to improve women's health, their scope and content have to be moulded by those involved in the promotion and protection of women's health. Otherwise the rights will remain abstract and inconsequential words that betray the hopes they inspire.

What is the nature of the State obligation?

The nature of State obligations to implement human rights with regard to women's health varies with the specific scope and content of each right in question and with the "general undertakings" accepted by a State under a particular human rights treaty. For example, a State's general obligation with respect to rights protected by the Political Covenant is immediate. Its "general undertaking" article (4) states:

> Each State Party to the present Covenant undertakes to respect and to ensure...the rights recognized in the present Covenant...

A State's obligation is "to respect" and "to ensure". A State complies with the duty to respect by not interfering with a right, but the obligation to ensure is substantially broader (54).

Rights under the Covenant are not only negative rights, in that States must not obstruct individual initiatives to take advantage of them, but also positive rights in that States must take steps to provide individuals with access to them. For example, an obligation to ensure rights might require States to take positive steps to discipline State health officials who have not adequately informed women of the occupational health hazards of State-owned businesses.

The character of the general obligations under the Economic Covenant (5) is both immediate and progressive:

> Each State Party to the present Covenant undertakes to take steps, individually and through international assistance and cooperation, especially economic and technical, to the maximum of its available resources, with a view to achieving progressively the full realization of the rights recognized in the present Covenant by all appropriate means, including particularly the adoption of legislative measures.

The undertaking "to take steps ... with a view to achieving progressively the full realization of the rights recognized" imposes obligations upon States Parties to act within a reasonable time. Steps towards full realization have to be taken immediately or shortly after ratification (55). For example, an obligation to take steps for the full realization of rights regarding health requires positive steps to address the most important preventable causes of women's premature death, such as maternal mortality. Where maternal mortality is low, States are obligated to address other factors of women's ill-health such as breast or cervical cancer.

The distinction commonly recognized between negative duties and positive duties of States reflects the distinction between individuals' negative and positive rights. A State's negative duty is a duty not to intervene in the exercise of individuals' rights. Breach of a negative duty is shown when a State has used an organ of government to intervene in or obstruct an individual's free pursuit of an entitlement. A positive duty requires a State to provide the means for individuals to achieve personal goals. A State's violation of a positive right may be shown in the State's failure to make an effort in good faith to provide the necessary resources to satisfy the right in question.

Legal interpretation will show whether a particular right requires States only not to intervene or only positively to provide services or whether the right is more complex in possessing both negative and positive aspects. For instance, the right to health protection against HIV infection has a negative aspect in that a State should not obstruct access to information about sources and means of prevention, but it also has a positive aspect in that the State should undertake public education about risk and prevention of infection.

Demonstration of a State's observance of both negative and positive human rights obligations will depend upon legal interpretation of the nature of the right and upon evidence of practice. Legal interpretation of a right concerns the terms of the treaty and the legally significant practice required to give effect to that right. State conformity with and breach of the human right can be shown by reference to events and statistics. An individual can prove occurrence of an event, such as State obstruction of access to a health service that is claimed to constitute unlawful interference with a negative right or denial of a service due as a positive right. States' observance or breach of duties to meet positive rights may be evidenced not only by incidents but also by reference to standards.

A State may satisfy a positive duty by making general provision of a health service without being required to meet each individual claim. A level of provision that satisfies an internationally determined standard demonstrates conformity with the treaty duty. In contrast, a State duty of non-interference with exercise of a human right may be shown violated by an instance of interference attributable to the State.

In terms of both positive duties to give effect to rights by meeting standards and negative duties of non-interference with individual pursuit of rights, States are obliged by general principles of international human rights law to advance the human rights to which they are committed. States must conform to standards of observance of both positive and negative duties in a way that satisfies the dynamic legal principle of progressive development towards the implementation of human rights. Standards of performance are expected to rise over time. State non-intervention in individuals' enjoyment of negative rights will be expected to become universal, if necessary through legislation that prohibits intervention or requires laws to be interpreted as subordinate to or compatible with such rights.

CHAPTER 4
International human rights to improve women's health

The following analysis of international human rights to improve women's health starts with the right to be free from all forms of discrimination and then addresses rights to survival, liberty and security of the person, the right to family and private life, rights regarding information and education, the right to health and health care, the right to the benefits of scientific progress and the rights regarding women's empowerment (see Annex 2). Examples are given of how each of these rights has been or could be applied to women's health problems. These rights may be applied differently in each country depending on the pattern of health services, the evolving understanding of health issues and perceptions of how women's ill-health can be prevented and treated in cost-effective ways.

The application of international human rights is explored through discrete and legally distinguishable categories of rights. Women's health interests often cross the boundaries that separate one legally described right from another. Advocates tend to invoke several rights that they allege have been jointly violated. They identify the specific articles of conventions that contain particular rights, and tribunals will distinguish one right from another in their judgements. However, approaches to women's health must refer to all of the several rights often implicated in a particular grievance.

The right of women to be free from all forms of discrimination

The Women's Convention (see Chapter 1) characterizes women's inferior status and oppression not just as a problem of inequality between men and women but rather as a function of sex and gender discrimination against women. The Convention is intended to be effective in liberating women to realize their individual and collective potential, and not merely to allow women to be brought to the same level of protection of rights that men enjoy. The Convention goes beyond the goal of non-discrimination between sexes, as required by the United Nations Charter, the Universal Declaration and its two implementing Covenants, and the three regional human rights treaties, to address the disadvantaged position of women in all areas of their lives, including health.

In contrast to previous human rights treaties, the Women's Convention frames the legal norm as the prohibition of all forms of discrimination against women, as distinct from the narrower norm of non-discrimination between sexes. That is, it develops the legal norm from a sex-neutral norm that requires equal treatment of men and women, usually measured by the scale of how men are treated, to recognize the fact that the nature of discrimination against women and their distinctive gender characteristics is worthy of a legal response. The Convention is thereby able to address the particular nature of the disadvantages that women suffer in diseases or conditions.

The definition in article 1 of the Women's Convention reads:

> ... the term "discrimination against women" shall mean any distinction, exclusion or restriction made on the basis of sex which has the effect or purpose of impairing or nullifying the recognition, enjoyment or exercise by women, irrespective of their marital status, on a basis of equality of men and women, of human rights and fundamental freedoms in the political, economic, social, cultural, civil or any other field.

Where the law makes a distinction that has the effect or purpose of impairing women's rights, it constitutes discrimination violating the Convention's definition and must accordingly be changed by the State Party. Discrimination against female gender offends the object and purpose of the Women's Convention.

The inclusion in the title of the Women's Convention of the phrase "all forms" emphasizes the determination described in paragraph 15 of its preamble to eliminate "such discrimination in all its forms and manifestations". The preamble expresses concern in paragraph 8 "that in situations of poverty women have the least access to food, health, education, training and opportunities for employment and other needs". As a result, the Convention entitles women to equal enjoyment with men not only of the so-called "first generation" of civil and political rights, such as the right to marry and found a family, but also of the "second generation" of economic, social and cultural rights, such as the right to health care.

The Women's Convention, in prohibiting all forms of discrimination, including private discrimination, is intended to be comprehensive. It recognizes that women are subject not only to specific, obvious inequalities but also to pervasive and subtle forms of sex and gender discrimination that are woven into the political, cultural and religious fabric of their societies. In addressing "all forms" of discrimination that women suffer, the Women's Convention requires States to confront the social causes of women's inequality in all systems, including the health system.

Article 12 of the Women's Convention prohibits all forms of discrimination against women in the delivery of health care. It provides:

1. States Parties shall take all appropriate measures to eliminate discrimination against women in the field of health care in order to ensure, on a basis of equality of men and women, access to health care services, including those related to family planning.

2. Notwithstanding the provisions of paragraph 1 of this article, States Parties shall ensure to women appropriate services in connection with pregnancy, confinement and the post-natal period, granting free services where necessary, as well as adequate nutrition during pregnancy and lactation.

Laws governing women's health should be scrutinized to ensure that they do not discriminate against women, by, for example, perpetuating negative or trivializing sex-role stereotypes that prevent women from being treated on their merits. Liability to pregnancy distinguishes women from men on biological grounds. Pregnancy-related disadvantages, such as exclusion from education, public office or employment (except when non-pregnancy is a bona fide work-related requirement), may accordingly be shown as illegally discriminatory against women because only women will suffer those disadvantages. Laws that deny or restrict women's access to health services, or make access dependent on another's authorization, impair women's rights. Such laws also impair women's power to protect their lives and health and to found families of a size and structure that best protect their health and that of their families. Laws restricting health services in this way can have a disadvantageous impact on women as opposed to men and can thereby constitute discrimination against women.

Some countries that have ratified the Women's Convention have moved to give effect to the Convention in domestic law. The Colombian Ministry of Public Health, for example, has recently interpreted the mandate of the Women's Convention to introduce into national health policies a gender perspective that considers "the social discrimination of women as an element which contributes to the ill-health of women" (56). To incorporate the Women's Convention into Colombian law (57, 58), article 12 on delivery of health care was made part of the country's new 1991 Constitution (59).

In Brazil in 1992 the State of São Paulo and many of its municipalities developed their own Convention based on the principles of the Women's Convention. This Convention, named the Paulista Convention on the Elimination of All Forms of Discrimination against Women, requires implementation of the Programme for Comprehensive Care of Women's Health. The programme emphasizes the need for a range of women's health services, including services for reproductive health, cancer prevention, menopause and old age, victimization by violence and, for example, for groups of women among whom conditions such as anaemia are of greater incidence. The programme also calls for measures to encourage normal birth and to fight the indiscriminate use of caesarean deliveries (60).

The removal of female stereotypes

Perhaps the greatest challenge faced in the improvement of women's health is the need to give effect to article 5(a) of the Women's Convention, by which States Parties commit themselves to take all appropriate measures:

> To modify the social and cultural patterns of conduct of men and women, with a view to achieving the elimination of prejudices and customary and all other practices which are based on the idea of the inferiority or the superiority of either of the sexes or on stereotyped roles for men and women.

Female genital mutilation, for instance, reflects a stereotypical perception that women may legitimately be exposed to non-therapeutic surgery in order to comply with the gender-specific norms of their community. While the sexes may rank equally as initiators of unchastity and adulterers may be equally condemned, loss of virginity is a greater stigma and barrier to marriage in women than in men, and men bear no health risks for premarital preservation of their virginity.

Article 5(a) points more widely to the need to examine such customs and might be used to require states both to educate those condoning and practising female genital mutilation on the record of its harmful effects (61, 62), and to use legal prohibitions where appropriate (63, 64).

Where food is scarce — whether due to poor agriculture, poor climate or the family's poor socioeconomic circumstances — the sequence of feeding often gives priority to males over females so that food goes first to a husband, then to sons, then to the mother and any daughters of the family. This practice may be reinforced in certain cultures where women see the survival of their husbands and sons as being of paramount importance to their own survival. Similarly, in some cultures newborn daughters are breast-fed for fewer months than sons. The incidence of malnutrition and anaemia in girls is directly related to rates of sickness and mortality.

The elimination of spousal authorization practices

Laws may often be formulated in ways that are disadvantageous to women's health. This may be because the motive of the laws is not promotion of health as such but preservation of another social value, such as the paternalistic protection of women's modesty. For example, spousal veto practices require a wife, but not a husband, to secure the authorization of her spouse in order to be physically examined for health care. This practice persists contrary to women's health interests and contrary to their right to be free from all forms of discrimination (65). It violates the Women's Convention and would accordingly have to be ended by a State applying the terms of that Convention.

Relevant ministries or departments of health might be encouraged to issue corrective regulations that stipulate that spousal authorization is not required by law, that it is contrary to rights to non-discrimination between sexes, and that it contravenes the professional ethics of health providers, who have obligations to safeguard women's health interests and to respect women's privacy and autonomy in resort to confidential health services. A regulation was issued by the Ministry of Health of Swaziland, pointing out that the practice of seeking the authorization of the client's spouse or relative "is contrary to the professionalism of the health worker" (65).

Rights to survival, liberty and security
The right to survival

The most obvious human right violated by avoidable death — not simply in pregnancy or childbirth but also as a cumulative result of health disadvantages — is a woman's right to life, also described as the right to survival. Article 6(1) of the Political Covenant provides that: "Every human being has the inherent right to life. This right shall be protected by law. No one shall be arbitrarily deprived of his life."[1]

This right has traditionally been discussed only in the legal context of the obligation of States Parties to ensure that courts observe due process of law before capital punishment is imposed (66). This understanding of the right to life is essentially male-oriented since men assimilate the imagery of capital punishment as more immediate to them than death from pregnancy or labour. Feminist legal approaches suggest that this inter-

---

[1] This article reflects article 3 of the Universal Declaration and is given further effect in, for instance, article 2 of the European Convention, article 4 of the American Convention and article 4 of the African Charter.

pretation of the right to life ignores the historical reality of women, which persists in regions of the world from which come almost all of the 500 000 women estimated to die each year from pregnancy-related causes. The Human Rights Committee established under the Political Covenant (67) has noted that:

> the right to life has been too often narrowly interpreted. The expression "inherent right to life" cannot be properly understood in a restrictive manner, and the protection of this right requires that states adopt positive measures.

The Committee considered it desirable that States Parties to the Political Covenant take all possible measures to reduce infant mortality and to increase life expectancy. A compatible goal is reduction of maternal mortality by, for instance, promotion of methods of birth spacing.

An argument that a woman's right to survival entitles her to access to appropriate health services (68, 69), and that legislation obstructing such access violates international human rights provisions (70), can be made with regard to an individual woman. The argument must be expanded, however, to apply where the threat to a woman's survival is indicated not by her individual medical condition but by her membership of a group at high risk of maternal mortality or morbidity. The collective right to survival of women in groups at risk raises the question of whether States have a positive obligation to offer these groups appropriate health services or, at least, education and counselling services that alert them both to risks and to means to minimize risks. The African Charter, given its emphasis on collective rights,[1] might well be invoked to impose obligations on African governments to give effect to rights of groups of individuals who are at highest risk of death through unintended pregnancies.

Rights to liberty and free and informed consent

Major abuses of women's liberty and autonomy occur in the delivery of health services, in part because of lack of enforcement and misapplication of the legal concept of informed consent. The manner in which a health service is offered and rendered can in some cases be a significant element in the service's success or failure to promote health. The strongest defence of individual integrity under the Political Covenant exists in article 9(1), which provides that:

---

[1] See, for example, the preamble and articles 4, 16, 18, 22 and 29 of the African Charter.

Everyone has the right to liberty and security of the person ... No one shall be deprived of his liberty except on such grounds and in accordance with such procedures as are established by law.[1]

A great deal can be done to improve the application of the principle of consent in order to ensure that women are provided with adequate information to decide on a proposed course of medical or other health treatment. The legal concept of informed consent is better understood as the right to make informed choices for one's own future. Even courts that have not accepted detailed doctrines about medical consent accept that medical choice involves individual liberty. The concept is an articulation of a broader ethical principle of respect for persons, which requires respect for the autonomy of competent individuals and protection of the vulnerable when they are incapable of making decisions, such as when a person is young or mentally handicapped (71).

The concept of informed consent to proposed treatment has two requirements, namely:

- that choice in health care be adequately informed;
- that consent to care be freely given or withheld.

The concept of "informed consent" is often used to cover both aspects of choice — informed consent or dissent and the right to uncoerced choice. The right to informed choice in health services, self-help and preventive health care is related to rights both to education and literacy and to rights to information and freedom of thought and association. The human rights of prospective recipients of health services have to be understood compatibly with the associated obligations of persons qualified to deliver health services.

Simple consent may consist only in agreement to comply with what is proposed. Such agreement is sometimes classified as "assent", as in the case of young persons who agree to be treated on the authorization of their parents. To exercise truly informed choice, a woman deciding whether to receive a health service must have sufficient understanding of:

- the proposed intervention;
- the implications of refusal of that treatment;
- alternative forms of management of her circumstances.

The role of information is to contribute to the individual's liberty to choose whether or not to accept a proposed form of management; it is

---

[1] This article reflects article 3 of the Universal Declaration and is given further effect in, for instance, article 2 of the European Convention, article 4 of the American Convention and article 4 of the African Charter.

not to persuade or condition a person to decide in a particular way, even if that way may appear to the health professional who gives the information to serve the person's best interests. In other words, the right to informed choice includes the right to make choices that health professionals may consider to be poor choices. Paternalistic medicine has been prone to conclude that women's choices are incompetently made if they do not follow health professionals' recommendations and that therefore women can be displaced as decision-makers concerning their medical treatment.

Information for the exercise of choice normally includes a fair description of the form of management proposed, as well as fair descriptions of alternatives to what is proposed (including postponing and not having any treatment), the known outcomes of each management option (i.e. their rates of successful outcome), the risks associated with each option (whether successful or not) and the likely effect of each form of management on the individual's lifestyle. Inadequate research into and understanding of the distinctive features of women's health and sickness have meant that the base of knowledge on which health professionals rest the information they give is not necessarily sensitive to women's health circumstances and requirements, and that proposed action may in fact aggravate women's health impairments. Research is needed to obtain health data specific to women in order to fulfil women's human rights to relevant information.

A major failure of personal liberty and autonomy specific to women occurs when a patient has not been adequately informed of the failure rate of a method of family planning she is thinking of accepting and when use of the method results in an unintended pregnancy or unintended infertility. Health professionals have ethical and legal duties to individuals to provide accurate information on contraceptive failure rates so that clients may make truly informed health choices about contraceptive methods.

The decision whether or not to accept medical treatment is not itself a medical decision. It is a personal decision unique to each individual. The individual must make the decision in accordance with her personality, likes and dislikes, comforts and discomforts, and goals in life as influenced by personal, family, social, philosophical and related perceptions. The role of health professionals is to give the individual decision-maker medical and other health-related information that contributes to the individual's power of choice and does not distort or unbalance that power.

Further, a woman must be free from coercion and over-inducement in exercising choice. The health professional giving information must not add to the pressures and hopes that the woman will naturally experience. Women seeking health services often feel dependent on care-givers.

Because they are reluctant to appear non-compliant or ungrateful, women frequently feel obliged to agree to whatever is proposed to them, particularly when those with the power of superior knowledge of medicine tell them that what is proposed is for their own good.

In order for women to exercise choice freely, they must act according to their own preferences. They should not be conditioned to comply with others' preferences by being dependent on current or future assistance for themselves or their families, and they should not feel obliged to undertake acts of self-sacrifice in order to pay for help they have received.

In Brazil, sterilization is legally available only for "therapeutic" reasons (72). A therapeutic reason is that a patient has had a surgical procedure. As a result, women may reluctantly choose caesarean sections for deliveries of children in order subsequently to meet the "therapeutic" requirement for sterilizations (73). This is ethically an unacceptable conditioning of women's choices of caesarean sections. The choice might be informed, but it is not free.

The conditioning of choice raises human rights concerns, not necessarily regarding any individual case but concerning the general capacity of women to control the medical choice of methods by which they deliver children. This is an area where indicators of percentages of natural and caesarean deliveries could be relevant.

Health professionals who provide improper counselling or treatment to individuals, and health professionals who wrongly withhold indicated treatment from patients for whom they are responsible, face three primary sources of legal liability (74):

- They may be charged with professional misconduct by the authorities that license them to practise and by any voluntary associations to which they belong and whose authority they have accepted to impose discipline for unethical professional behaviour.
- Where they have touched a person in a way that lacks legal authorization, or that exceeds authorization, or that differs from what was authorized, they may be sued for compensation for battery (or unauthorized touching) and/or they may be prosecuted for related crimes of assault.
- Where they have failed to make appropriate disclosures to patients whose informed choices they were required to facilitate and obtain, they may be sued for negligence. Negligence arises in law where health professionals fail to meet the legal standard of disclosure of information, resulting in their patients suffering injuries they would have escaped had different choices been made. Health professionals are often required to provide information relevant to the choices that women have to make.

Legal remedies to reinforce duties to treat patients with respect and care often serve no more than symbolic purposes. In many countries, the formal procedures of the law are in fact inaccessible to many people and the mechanisms of health service licensing authorities and professional associations are similarly beyond reach. States themselves may bear responsibility under international human rights law, and be accountable before international tribunals and agencies, if they authorize or permit delivery of health services that are beyond the control of the recipients. This may particularly be the case where providers of health services are not accountable to provide compensation or other remedies for violations of the human rights of health service recipients or those denied care.

A normal legal precondition to State responsibility is that individual complainants must first have resort to national tribunals and must exhaust local remedies before matters can be taken up at international level. States must be given an opportunity through their legal systems to correct wrongs to individuals. Where local remedies do not exist, however, or where they are inaccessible, State responsibility may be directly involved at international level.

Discussion of compensation or other remedies before local courts may seem unrealistic in many circumstances. Yet if domestic remedies are inaccessible, States are more directly accountable under international human rights law for wrongs in delivery of health services that are violations of human rights.

Where individual compensation is accessible, the disadvantaged position of women may be compounded and underscored. The basis of financial compensation is normally to put a patient in the position she would have been in had the wrong not occurred, in so far as the difference can be calculated in monetary terms. This measure of compensation usually requires a complainant to show on a balance of probabilities that, had the health service been properly rendered, she would have enjoyed a health advantage.

A party accused of wrongdoing may propose the defence that the patient's overall circumstances were so compromised or inadequate that she cannot show that she would have been better off had a wrong not occurred. Accordingly, unless a complainant can show that a health service would have made a difference to her life span and her ability to function, her claim may not warrant compensation. The position is worse when the complaint is that death resulted, since where mortality levels are high it may not be possible to show that a woman in the victim's health circumstances was likely to survive.

The right to security of the person

In its widest sense, the right to security is equal to the right to well-being and coincides with the WHO understanding of health. Health contributes to security and security is a major component of health. In international human rights law, considerations for evaluation of security include the power of informed choice. Insecurity reflects not just a lack of health and resources but vulnerability to become disadvantaged. Security is addressed in straightforward terms in the first sentence of article 7 of the Political Covenant, which provides that:

> No one shall be subjected to torture or to cruel, inhuman or degrading treatment or punishment.

How this provision applies to medical interventions and to denial of desired medical care is seen in the second and last sentence of article 7, which provides that:

> In particular, no one shall be subjected without his free consent to medical or scientific experimentation.

Even without regard to experimentation, the denial of health care and the imposition of an unwanted health status appear cruel. More pervasive insecurity is generated, however, by degrading treatment of women, such as occurs when they are treated as inferior and when preservation of their lives and health is regarded as a low priority in the allocation of health care resources.

Human rights law and practice have tended to focus on security against deliberately inflicted harm. Much violence against women, which endangers and reduces their enjoyment of their lives, occurs within women's own homes at the hands of those for whom they care and who often claim to care for them.

Exposure to violence can begin in childhood, in both sexual and non-sexual ways. Article 19 of the Children's Convention requires States:

> to protect the child from all forms of physical or mental violence, injury or abuse, neglect or negligent treatment, maltreatment or exploitation, including sexual abuse.

Girls are specially vulnerable since their principal values often appear, paradoxically, to be their sexual availability and their chastity. Preservation of virginity before marriage through circumcision denies girl children security against the known physical and mental consequences of female genital mutilation (28, 29, 61, 62). Health dangers are also associated with obstacles to termination of pregnancies of young girls, whether inside or outside marriage.

Rights to family and private life
The right to marry and found a family (75)

Article 23 of the Political Covenant and article 10 of the Economic Covenant both recognize the family as the "natural and fundamental group unit of society". The former states that "the right of men and women of marriageable age to marry and found a family shall be recognized."[1] The latter recognizes that "special protection should be accorded to mothers during a reasonable period before and after childbirth. During such period working mothers should be accorded paid leave or leave with adequate social security benefits" (5).

The Human Rights Committee's General Comments on article 23 of the Political Covenant (76) explain that:

> The right to found a family implies, in principle, the possibility to procreate and live together. When States Parties adopt family planning policies, they should be compatible with the provisions of the Covenant and should, in particular, not be discriminatory or compulsory.

The right to found a family is inadequately observed if it amounts to no more than the right to conceive, gestate and deliver a child.

An act of "foundation" goes beyond a passive submission to biology. It involves the right of a woman positively to plan, time and space the births of children so as to maximize their health and her own (77). Article 16(1)(e) of the Women's Convention requires States Parties to ensure that women enjoy:

> [equal] rights to decide freely and responsibly on the number and spacing of their children and to have access to the information, education and means to enable them to exercise these rights.

At its 1994 meeting, the Committee on the Elimination of Discrimination against Women (CEDAW) adopted a General Recommendation on

---

[1] This article reflects article 16 of the Universal Declaration and is given further effect in, for instance, article 12 of the European Convention, article 17 of the American Convention and article 18 of the African Charter.

equality in marriage and family relations. In relation to article 16(1)(*e*) of the Women's Convention, CEDAW stated:

> The responsibilities that women have to bear and raise children affect their right of access to education, employment and other activities related to their personal development. They also impose inequitable burdens of work on women. The number and spacing of their children have a similar impact on women's lives and also affect their physical and mental health, as well as that of their children. For these reasons, women are entitled to decide on the number and spacing of their children.

> Some reports disclose coercive practices which have serious consequences for women, such as forced pregnancies, abortions or sterilization. Decisions to have children or not, while preferably made in consultation with spouse or partner, must not nevertheless be limited by spouse, parent, partner or Government. In order to make an informed decision about safe and reliable contraceptive measures, women must have information about contraceptive measures and their use, and guaranteed access to sex education and family planning services, as provided in article 10(h) of the Convention.

> There is general agreement that where there are freely available appropriate measures for the voluntary regulation of fertility, the health, development and well-being of all members of the family improve. Moreover, such services improve the general quality of life and health of the population, and the voluntary regulation of population growth helps preserve the environment and achieve sustainable economic and social development.

In commenting on article 16(1)(*e*) of the Women's Convention, CEDAW explained that "women's right to full and free exercise of their reproductive functions, including the right to decide whether to have children or not, must not be limited by spouse or government, and women must also be guaranteed access to information about safe contraceptive methods, sex education and family planning services" (*78, 79*).

One Latin American country has adopted a new ministerial resolution that orders all health institutions to ensure that women have the right to decide on all issues affecting their health, their lives and their sexuality (*80*). The resolution guarantees rights "to information and orientation to allow the exercise of free, gratifying, responsible sexuality which can not be tied to maternity." The new policy requires provision of a full range of reproductive health services, including infertility services, safe and effective contraception, integrated treatment for incomplete abortion and, for example, treatment for menopausal women. The policy emphasizes the

31

need for special attention to high-risk women such as adolescents and victims of violence.

In some parts of the world, the right to found a family is most threatened by reproductive tract infections. In Africa, for example, reproductive tract infections cause up to 50% of infertility (*81, 82*). Government inaction to prevent or remedy this source of infertility violates the right to found a family. This is so whether or not the right is classified in law as a positive right, i.e. a right that governments must serve through positive action. If the right is negative, in that a State must not obstruct its exercise by those who are capable of founding their families without reliance on State action, legal liability of the State for inaction might nevertheless arise not because of infertility itself but because of the differential impact that infertility has on the lives of women (*83*).

The right to found a family incorporates the right to maximize the survival prospects of a conceived or existing child, which can be done through birth spacing and other family planning methods. This right is complementary to the woman's right to survive pregnancy, for instance by delaying a first pregnancy.

State laws that do not provide a minimum age for marriage, and practices that do not enforce such laws, permit young girls to marry — not uncommonly with questionably free consent — and to conceive children before they are physiologically mature. This results in high rates of maternal and infant mortality and high levels of morbidity, such as vesico-vaginal fistulae.

The right to marry and to found a family can be limited by laws that are reasonably related to family-based objectives. Laws requiring a minimum age for marriage are not incompatible with the right to marry and to found a family. The right to marry and to be a parent is a right of adults rather than of children or young adolescents. Indeed, an objection to many age of marriage laws is that they set an age that is too low for the welfare of women, and therefore of their families, and that they set lower ages for women than for men. Women are frequently induced to marry at the minimum legal age, or a lower age through non-enforcement of or exceptions to the law, in part because of lack of alternative opportunities in life.

Parental support obligations may legally terminate at the age of marriage, after which women may have no means to support themselves and no opportunities to pursue education or careers. Young women are accordingly led to early marriage and childbearing by socioeconomic and cultural influences that recognize no function or worth of women except as wives and mothers. Human rights provisions that no one shall be obliged involuntarily to enter marriage fail to recognize that many women "volunteer" for marriage through lack of any dignified alternative following adolescence.

The right to private and family life

The American Convention on Human Rights implies the right to privacy in its article 11, which provides that:

> Everyone has the right to have his honor respected and his dignity recognized.

Honour and dignity are private attributes that government has no interest to diminish.

The right to private and family life is distinguishable from the right to found a family, although for some purposes the latter right may be considered to be part of the former. The right to private and family life contains liberty interests. Article 17 of the Political Covenant provides that:

> No one shall be subjected to arbitrary or unlawful interference with his privacy, family, home or correspondence, nor to unlawful attacks on his honour and reputation.[1]

The European Convention specifies conditions under which private and family life may be compromised or sacrificed to higher interests of the state, including interests in public health. Article 8 provides that:

> 1. Everyone has the right to respect for his private and family life, his home and his correspondence.
>
> 2. There shall be no interference by a public authority with the exercise of this right except such as is in accordance with the law and is necessary in a democratic society in the interests of national security, public safety or the economic well-being of the country, for the prevention of disorder or crime, for the protection of health or morals, or for the protection of the rights and freedoms of others.

In a case in Western Europe two women claimed that a restrictive abortion law interfered with respect for their private lives contrary to this article, in that they were not permitted privately and alone to decide to terminate their unwanted pregnancies (84). The majority of the European Commission on Human Rights rejected the applicants' claim, however,

---

[1] This article reflects article 12 of the Universal Declaration and is given further effect in, for instance, article 11 of the American Convention and articles 4 and 5 of the African Charter.

and found that the restrictive law did not constitute an interference with private life.

Greater scope was given to a woman's right to private life in another case in Europe (85). The European Commission on Human Rights upheld a national judicial decision protecting a woman from being compelled to continue an unwanted pregnancy through her husband's legal power of veto of her abortion. The Commission gave priority to respect for a wife's private life and integrity in her decision on childbearing over her husband's right to respect for his family life in the birth of his child. The Commission found that the husband's right could not be interpreted to embrace even a legal right to be consulted on his wife's decision. A State's interest in an unborn life is not greater than that of the biological father's, so that preclusion of his right appears to preclude the State's right to prevail, at least up to some advanced stage of pregnancy.

Rights to information and education

Rights to seek, receive and impart information are protected by all the basic human rights conventions, and are essential to the realization of women's health. Information concerns health services that may be available by health authorities' choice or obligation, means of self-help and preventive health care. Medical organizations at times oppose availability of information on the grounds that "quack" medicine is harmful and deters recourse to proven therapies. Some unproven treatments are indeed later proven harmful, and regulation of unproven treatments may be defensible when regulators can show a credible risk of harm to the unwary.

Sometimes, however, information is prohibited on moral grounds, as shown in the history of information regarding treatment of reproductive tract infections and in family planning. The Women's Convention explicitly requires in article 10(h) that women have the right:

> to specific educational information to help to ensure the health and well-being of families, including information and advice on family planning.

Article 10(1) of the European Convention provides that:

> the right to freedom of expression shall include freedom ... to receive and impart information and ideas without interference by public authority and regardless of frontiers.

In a case before the European Court of Human Rights in 1992 (86), the Court ruled that a national ban on counselling women on where to obtain abortions abroad violated this article. In order to comply with this decision, national law could not prohibit counselling of women on where to find reproductive health services in other countries. This was despite the fact that these services could not be rendered lawfully in the country where the counselling was prohibited. This decision applies to States Parties to the European Convention that try to restrict the counselling of women seeking health services in other countries.

The right to education serves the goal of individual and public health. Women who are literate have easier access to health information since they can read and understand about risks to their health and how to prevent them.

Questions concerning the human rights of students may arise when schools exclude medical instruction on sexual health. Both education and deliberate silence affecting schooling in sexual matters can raise conflicts between rights to freedom of thought and rights to religious observance, including instruction in religious values.

Controversy has arisen when public school systems have introduced health-oriented or family health programmes to which parents and religious organizations have objected because the sexual content of instruction offended their religious convictions.

In another case in Europe, some parents took exception to compulsory sex education in State schools. They complained that it violated the State's duty to respect "the right of parents to ensure such education and teaching in conformity with their own religious and philosophical convictions" (6), and violated their right to religious non-discrimination, rights to private and family life, and/or the right to freedom of thought, conscience and religion set out in the European Convention.

The European Court of Human Rights held that compulsory sex education classes in State schools violated none of these duties or rights because the classes were primarily intended to convey useful and corrective information which, though unavoidably concerned with considerations of a moral nature, did not exceed "the bounds of what a democratic state may regard as in the public interest".

The Court recognized, however, that

the State ... must take care that information or knowledge included in the curriculum is conveyed in an objective, critical and pluralistic manner. The State is forbidden to pursue an aim of indoctrination that might be considered as not respecting parents' religious and philosophical convictions (87).

The right to health and health care

By article 12(1) of the Economic Covenant, States Parties "recognize the right of everyone to the enjoyment of the highest attainable standard of physical and mental health". Article 12(2) provides that the steps to achieve the full realization of this right shall include those necessary for:

> (a) The provision for the reduction of the stillbirth-rate and of infant mortality and for the healthy development of the child ...

> (d) The creation of conditions which would assure to all medical service and medical attention in the event of sickness.[1]

This article is reinforced by article 24(1)(f) of the Children's Convention, which requires States Parties to "develop preventive health care, guidance for parents and family planning education and services". Article 12(1) of the Women's Convention requires that States Parties "eliminate discrimination against women in the field of health care in order to ensure, on a basis of equality of men and women, access to health care services, including those related to family planning".

Through ratification of international human rights treaties and through national constitutions and laws, governments commit themselves to protect their populations' rights to health care. The right to health care is compromised when women's protection of their well-being is obstructed by barriers that are governmentally, legislatively or judicially constructed. Beyond impairing women's provision to themselves of desired health care, governments may fail to provide necessary health services to women who for various reasons cannot make provision for themselves — for instance because of lack of knowledge, or because of poverty or their remoteness from main population centres. Obstruction of available health services and non-provision of reasonable access to otherwise unavailable health services deny women the right to health care that countries have acknowledged through their acceptance of international human rights treaties.

General comment on women's right to health

Treaty bodies have the power to make General Comments or General Recommendations to indicate ways in which States Parties should interpret and apply the respective treaties. These detailed comments can be

---

[1] This article reflects article 25 of the Universal Declaration and is given further effect in, for instance, article 13 of the European Social Charter, article 26 of the American Convention and article 10 of its Additional Protocol in the Area of Economic, Social and Cultural Rights, article 16 of the African Charter and article 24 of the Children's Convention.

particularly useful for elaborating the specific content of broadly worded treaty guarantees. For example, the General Recommendations of CEDAW indicate the kind of information that States should provide in their periodic reports to CEDAW in accordance with the Women's Convention. These recommendations, which include recommendations on women and AIDS and on female circumcision, establish indicators and criteria by which to measure governments' observance of their international duties to give effect to the rights of women. States are given latitude to choose the means to achieve those goals.

To date, the International Labour Organisation (ILO) is the only specialized agency of the United Nations that has provided expert advice to CEDAW on the substance and working of the General Recommendations relating to women and work (*88*). ILO, unlike most of the specialized agencies, integrates its development work with its human rights activities and provides assistance to most human rights treaty bodies on setting standards and putting them into effect. WHO is giving consideration to providing similar assistance to CEDAW. It should be noted that WHO is already integrating its development and human rights work with respect to the Convention on the Rights of the Child, including support to the Committee and its reporting functions.

While the global indicators for health for all are relevant to the right to health care, they are intended for use in obtaining a global overview and not in measuring State compliance with the right to health care as protected by human rights treaties. Moreover, WHO has indicated that the development of national strategies aimed at achieving greater social equity in health status would require the disaggregation of carefully selected indicators (*89*). Wider consultation between those involved in the fields of health and human rights will help to identify key measures for determining State compliance with treaty obligations relating to the promotion and protection of women's health.

Principles for the promotion and protection of women's health

The development of principles for the promotion and protection of women's health is another approach that might be considered. Such principles could draw on national women's health policies and experience in the development of the Principles for the Protection of Persons with Mental Illness and for the Improvement of Mental Health Care (*90*) which were prepared under the auspices of the Commission on Human Rights in close collaboration with WHO and adopted by the United Nations General Assembly. Principles on the promotion and protection of women's health could address, but not necessarily be limited to, the following issues:

Health status factors

- health considerations important to women at different stages of their life cycle;
- the need to determine the special impact on women of routine health procedures and products;
- the importance of improving research on women's health requirements;
- the need to consider women's health requirements and circumstances in the development of research protocols;
- the importance of basing health policies on the most up-to-date scientific and technological knowledge;

Health service factors

- the importance of treating women with dignity and respect, including the provision of adequate information so that women can make informed decisions on particular courses of treatment;
- the rights of women as patients and the importance of confidentiality and privacy;

Conditions affecting the health and well-being of women

- the importance of ensuring a healthy and safe working environment;
- the importance of eliminating traditions and practices that have detrimental health consequences for women;
- the ability to identify and respond appropriately to women who live in abusive environments.

The above list is merely suggestive of the kinds of issues that could be addressed in order to incorporate human rights relevant to women's health into health policies and health care practices. Clearly, wider consultation is needed among women and those knowledgeable about women's health, human rights and medical ethics for the development of principles for the promotion and protection of women's health.

Women's health care laws

Perhaps based upon principles for the promotion and protection of women's health, a set of guidelines might be developed for the legal promotion of women's health in particular areas, such as women's occupational health, the health of girl children and reproductive health care. Health legislation has contributed substantially to the promotion of public health, and could be used more vigorously to promote women's health.

For example, guidelines for comprehensive reproductive health laws may be particularly important in view of legal impediments to women's access to reproductive health services. Such laws would encourage reduction of pregnancy-related deaths and sickness, and would provide services that promote reproductive health. United Nations documentation draws on extensive worldwide evidence to reach the conclusion that "the ability to regulate the timing and number of births is one central means of freeing women to exercise the full range of human rights to which they are entitled" (91).

Women's right to control their fertility through the prohibition of all forms of discrimination against women may therefore be a fundamental key that opens up women's capacity to enjoy other human rights and to achieve the physical, mental and social well-being that is the essence of health (70).

A strategy for a comprehensive reproductive health law that could facilitate and maximize reproductive health has been proposed (92):

> A responsive reproductive health care strategy would attend to the reproductive health needs of all, by providing education for responsible and safe sex life, contraception for the sexually active to use as needed, and services for the management of pregnancy, delivery, and all abortion. It would also provide education and services for the prevention and management of STDs, subfertility and infertility. Its goal should be to make human sexuality and reproduction a joy, not a curse or a punishment.

This strategy is reflected in Recommendation 4 of the International Conference on Better Health for Women and Children through Family Planning (93):

> Unwanted pregnancy should be recognized as a specific health risk for women and their families. Regardless of the legal status, humane treatment of septic and incomplete abortion and post-abortion contraceptive advice and services should be made available. The magnitude of the problem and its implications for the health of women and families should be documented and publicized. Where legal, good-quality abortion services should be made easily accessible to all women.

It has been pointed out by some that enactment of a comprehensive reproductive health care law would greatly facilitate women's human rights to health care. It would provide an opportunity to move the legal regulation of women's reproductive health into the realm of social justice where women are treated with dignity and respect (94, 95, 96, 97).

Many countries with criminal laws prohibiting services for contraception, voluntary sterilization, abortion, sexually transmitted diseases and infertility have high rates of maternal mortality and morbidity, often associated with repeated pregnancies and unskilled, including self-induced, abortions. Such criminal laws are also associated with socio-economic inequities. Persons with private means to avail themselves of reproductive health services will do so, perhaps in foreign countries where high-quality services are legally available, but those dependent on public provision of health services will face the physical, economic and social consequences of clandestine abortion and, for instance, infertility associated with poor reproductive health and unsafe abortion (98).

Where the practice of medicine requires that competent account be taken of the impact on women's health, the laws should apply the WHO definition of health.

The right to the benefits of scientific progress

Article 15(1)(b) of the Economic Covenant recognizes the right of everyone "to enjoy the benefits of scientific progress and its applications". Further, under article 15(3), States Parties "undertake to respect the freedom indispensable for scientific research ...".[1] To ensure that women have access to the benefits of scientific progress, research on diseases and conditions that exclusively or primarily affect women will be necessary. Research needs will vary according to countries and regions, depending on the prevailing patterns of mortality and morbidity. In some countries, for instance, research may be necessary to understand nutritional patterns that maximize a woman's chances of preventing breast cancer. In other instances, research may be necessary to develop a better understanding of osteoporosis or fertility control or the causes of infertility. Freedom of research requires States Parties to accommodate such research and development, designed particularly from women's perspectives (99).

In order to ensure that women can take advantage of the right to the benefits of scientific progress, some medical institutions are beginning to initiate policies to ensure that scientific research produces results that are specifically relevant to women, in part as a result of the encouragement of nongovernmental organizations (NGOs) (100). For example, in the United States since 1986 the National Institutes of Health and the Alcohol, Drug Abuse, and Mental Health Administration have required that clinical research findings should be of benefit to all persons at risk, regardless of sex (101).

Once scientific research opens the way to better understanding of female physiology and anatomy and, for example, the causes of women's

---

[1] This article reflects article 27(2) of the Universal Declaration.

poor health, the right to the benefits of scientific progress requires that women have access to treatments and technologies based on the results of scientific research.

The responsibility of States Parties to the Economic Covenant to ensure respect for access to the benefits of scientific progress might in part be met through the enactment of what are called "use it or lose it" patent provisions governing therapeutic, diagnostic and preventive health care products (102). When product patents have been granted to sponsors who subsequently fail or decline to market such products that are beneficial to health, government authorities in several countries, such as France (103), have the legal power to transfer the patents to new holders who will undertake marketing of the products. In conferring a patent on a drug manufacturer, a government is giving the manufacturer a monopoly to market a therapeutic product. In return, the government expects a health benefit for its population. The potential for involuntary transfer of a patent from a manufacturer who fails to make the product available acknowledges that a drug patent serves not only the commercial interests of the holder but also the interest of government in the health of potential users.

Rights regarding women's empowerment

The poor state of women's health in many regions of the world, including within deprived socioeconomic populations in developed countries, can be seen as one result of women's inability to protect their own interests and those of groups in which women form a majority.

Decisions to exercise individual power or to participate in the exercise of collective power are attributes of liberty and autonomy. In many settings, women have never enjoyed autonomy, the conviction that they can act autonomously, or the belief that they rightfully should be influential in the circumstances that affect their health. Principles of international human rights are available to women who want to take responsibility for their individual health and for the well-being of women in their communities. Many basic human rights and freedoms, which many countries of the world find dignity in accepting, provide women with psychological and legal instruments of empowerment. These rights to empowerment may be employed by women to realize their own health goals.

The right to freedom of religion and thought

The right to freedom of religion and thought is contained in most human rights treaties. Leaders of the religious, political and cultural institutions that define acceptable status and roles for women have traditionally been men. The goal of women's better health affords women a benign and

41

sympathetic justification for presenting their communities with the need to think afresh about adherence to oppressive practices. The backdrop of women's poor health provides advocates of women's improved health with a convincing stage for action.

The tenets of religious faith need not be repudiated in order to characterize wrongs to women's health as unacceptable. The United Nations (*104*) has adopted the position that:

> states should condemn violence against women and should not invoke any custom, tradition or religious consideration to avoid their obligations with respect to its elimination.

Religious doctrines neither require nor condone violence as such, but religious texts may be cited in support of practices and social institutions whose consequences endanger the health of women (*20*). Women are entitled to invoke freedom from the effects of such interpretations of religious texts and to adhere to alternative understandings.

The right to freedom of assembly and association

Frequently relevant to freedom of thought and to empowerment is the right to meet with others and to identify oneself with their causes, convictions and activities. The entitlement of like-minded people to gather and collaborate has been established through claims of rights of religious and political assembly and association. Regarding women's health, women can claim freedom to meet with others to learn about threats to health and means of prevention and protection. Many provisions on the advertising of contraceptive methods and on control of sexually transmitted diseases and abortion are located in criminal laws among sections addressing public morality and decency. Rights of assembly and association with communicators of health knowledge may be invoked to measure these provisions and laws against the standards of international human rights.

The right to political participation

The right to political participation allows women and women's health groups to inform government of their experiences of unsatisfactory and inadequate health services and to present proposals for reform. The right to participation to enhance women's health is at best a means to the end rather than an end in itself. Its utility to government and to the quality of public life is that it may offer women a reasonable prospect of discourse and may disclose facts and perceptions that government investigators overlook, devalue or omit from reports. It is for advocates of improved health for women to determine to what extent the right to political participation is adequately available in their circumstances, to what extent the right is effective and to what extent it is a priority among options for advocacy and action.

CHAPTER 5
Human rights mechanisms for protection of women's health

International human rights law depends for its effective application on international consensus and the implementation of effective means of action. Facts about disregard for the poor state of women's health indicate that solemn undertakings to observe human rights have been violated. States do not readily agree on what constitutes discrimination against women. Some hold that societal roles assigned to women on religious or cultural grounds that separate the roles of women from those of men do not fall within the ambit of discrimination; others disagree. It might be easier to develop consensus on the need to advance women's health because of the stark testimony of the health risks associated with women's poor status.

Methods of protection of women's health rights range from recourse to limited international and regional judicial or quasi-judicial processes to the application of broader means of furthering accountability of States, such as through reporting requirements under international and regional human rights treaties to which they are parties (105). The application of human rights law at all levels is needed to develop consensus and to crystallize the content of human rights relevant to women's health. Any one method may be fragile and inadequate, but there are cumulative ways in which consensus can be developed about the need to remedy the injustices associated with the neglect of women's health.

International protection

State compliance with treaty obligations to implement human rights is monitored by the committees established under the various treaties. The members of these committees serve in their capacity as experts and not as representatives of governments. States Parties are required to make periodic reports to the treaty bodies on the steps they have taken to implement their obligations and on the difficulties they have experienced. Reports are examined by the relevant treaty committees in the presence of representatives of the States concerned. Committees usually also receive information from NGOs about State compliance with the treaties, which some committee members will use in their questioning of State representatives. If members of a treaty body are strongly critical of a State, or express the view that the State has not discharged its obligations under the treaty, consideration may have to be given to mechanisms to ensure implementation of these obligations where health is concerned.

In addition to the treaty-based bodies, there are United Nations bodies that are established under the United Nations Charter that provide opportunities for exposure of the injustice of the neglect of women's health.

The Commission on the Status of Women meets annually and is composed of government representatives from Member countries. It is an important international forum for advancement of women's status, particularly for Member countries that are not parties to human rights treaties. This Commission has had input to the International Year for the World's Indigenous People, 1993, the World Conference on Human Rights, 1993, the International Conference on Population and Development and the International Year of the Family, 1994, and the World Summit for Social Development, 1995. The Commission also acts as preparatory committee for the Fourth World Conference on Women, 1995.

The Sub-Commission on Prevention of Discrimination and Protection of Minorities of the Commission on Human Rights has used working groups and special rapporteurs to address alleged human rights violations where women are particularly vulnerable. The Sub-Commission created, for example, a Special Rapporteur on Traditional Practices Affecting the Health of Women and Children and, at its 1994 session, the Commission on Human Rights appointed a Special Rapporteur on Violence Against Women. The Commission on Human Rights provides another forum in which general principles for the promotion and protection of women's health might be advanced. It is important to recognize the invaluable and increasing role which NGOs play, in collaboration with agencies of the United Nations system, in the protection and promotion of health as a human right and of women's health in particular. The United Nations appointed its first High Commissioner for Human Rights in February 1994.

Regional protection

Regional human rights conventions have been applied only sparingly to violations of women's rights (106, 107, 108, 109, 110), and even less to rights regarding women's health. There are opportunities at regional level, however, that do not necessarily exist at international level for the promotion and protection of women's health. Geographical proximity, cultural similarity and economic interdependence can all facilitate the regional development and application of human rights standards (*111*) to women's health. Advocates are just beginning to use regional human rights systems to establish legitimacy of women's rights within regional cultures, and a great deal can be done to use these systems for the promotion and protection of women's health.

Some of the regional systems have specific organs dealing with women's rights that can be used to great effect to advance rights regarding women's health. The Council of Europe, for instance, has a Steering Committee for Equality between Women and Men, and the Organization of American States has a Commission on Women.

National protection: human rights responsibilities of the health professions
Ethical guidelines

A characteristic often ascribed to practitioners of professions is that they must confront and resolve ethical problems. Practitioners who are conscious of the distinctive planes of microethics (person-to-person ethics) and macroethics (group-to-group and group-to-individual ethics) are likely to identify more ethical problems in their practices than their colleagues who remain unaware of the issues involved. The patronizing attitudes that health professionals may have towards women patients present microethical concerns. Women's lack of access to practitioners raises macroethical problems of resource allocation.

Codes of ethical conduct deal more easily and perhaps more successfully with microethical concerns, such as patients' consent to treatment and confidentiality. However, some traditional professional codes still presume that health protection and restoration have priority over the autonomy of patients to exercise choice in ways that may be counter-therapeutic. Health professionals inspired by the mandate to do no harm are challenged to serve patients whose choices the professionals consider ill-advised.

Medical management that may compromise women's health, such as resort to caesarean deliveries upon mere speculation of fetal distress and prescription of dependence-producing drugs to women without thorough diagnoses and consideration of alternatives, are rarely measured against codes of ethical conduct. This is due in part to women's incapacity to compel enforcement of ethical codes, often because of unawareness that codes and monitoring mechanisms exist. But it is also due to the fact that abuse becomes apparent not in case-by-case management of individual patients but through comparative epidemiological or population-based studies. For instance, a caesarean delivery may be an appropriate option in an individual labour, but if the rate of such deliveries in a given population vastly exceeds that in neighbouring populations of comparable health status, with comparable profiles of maternal and infant risk, this may suggest an unregulated style of local medical practice that overutilizes this intervention. Respect for the ethical principles of justice, beneficence and patients' informed autonomy may require associations of specialists or general physicians to monitor and report comparative practice.

Advocates of improved health for women can usefully observe the diligence with which associations of health professionals scrutinize the ethical conduct of their members under present codes and may invoke women's human rights to require refinement or amplification of such codes for the sake of improvement of women's health. The fact that a form of health care practice meets the standards of existing law does not in itself answer the question of whether the practice is ethical. Observance of ethics and human rights may require conduct that meets more than the strict letter or minimum standards of the law. The development of specific ethical guidance for the promotion and protection of women's health might be a creative first step. The inclusion of such guidance in an ethical code will not alone be sufficient to ensure ethical practice of health professionals and their respect for human rights. Education and training are needed, as are mechanisms to strengthen professional accountability.

Education and training

The practices that students of the health professions may experience in training also reinforce codes of conduct. Training for practice in a health profession requires instruction not only in technique and dexterity but also in sensitivity and ethical responsibilities both to patients and to the profession itself. Just how ethically educational institutions and professional bodies themselves recruit students of both sexes and, for instance, from minority groups, is an important question. This is particularly the case in light of the historical view of institutional medicine that its study and practice were not suitable for women, and the stereotypical belief that nursing practice is a "feminine" and subordinate occupation that serves physicians.

Instruction in awareness of the human rights of patients should be given by both precept and example and should be pitched at the levels of both clinical practice and service to communities. For instance, students need to be familiar with differential impacts of approaches and techniques on the two sexes.

Strengthening professional accountability

Associations of health professionals should take initiatives to ensure that their members have relevant information about the distinctive physiological, psychological and social features of women's health, and that they treat women patients with appropriate regard for their circumstances. For instance, women patients should not be treated as children, nor should questioning or examinations that are necessary for their health care be avoided for fear of indelicacy. Associations should equip their members to meet standards of respect for human rights, should monitor members' training in principles of human rights relevant to improving women's health and should hold them accountable for their failures.

A distinction may be recognized between professional licensing or regulatory authorities and voluntary associations of health care practitioners with common interests in professional education, protection and advancement. The former usually have legal power to compel professional accountability through disciplinary action for proven misconduct. They can impose penalties, such as withdrawal of professional status or suspension from practice. The latter may create tribunals to adjudicate continuing membership but do not have more powers over members than members agree to grant. Voluntary associations can suspend or expel members but such members remain licensed practitioners. Nevertheless, whether membership is a legal precondition to professional practice or a voluntary gesture of solidarity with the goals of professional peers, associations of health professionals taking initiatives to create and improve commitment to women's improved health and health care may find reinforcement in the principles of international human rights. A condition of the associations' credibility, of course, is that they admit women to licensure and membership without discrimination, and are open to the contributions that women can make to professional education and sensitivity.

CHAPTER 6
Conclusion

International human rights relevant to women's health are worth little where there are no enforceable duties to make them effective. In fact, international, regional and national legal instruments and institutions offer a variety of opportunities to establish standards for observance of human rights and to hold States to account for levels of respect for human rights that prevail within their territories. Failures to enforce standards of observance may be due in part to institutional defects, but may be due in larger part to lack of initiatives to use available legal mechanisms to identify the low health status of women that constitutes a violation of international human rights law, to enforce legal remedies for violations and to require maintenance of legal standards.

One product of the empowerment of women is likely to be resort to legal institutions that scrutinize State conduct and measure performance against international standards of protection and promotion of women's health. A variety of agencies may create initiatives to hold States to account for their human rights record. With regard to women's rights to health care, however, agencies at all levels require personnel familiar with the principles and machinery of international human rights law who can also use women's health data to demonstrate both violations of rights and conforming practices. In the past, the inspiration of human rights values has not been applied to women's health and the quest to serve women's health has not been informed by awareness of internationally recognized claims to respect for human rights.

Current initiatives exist to enhance women's health through human rights law. At the national level, health care associations are providing legal services to women to educate them about their legal rights and to advance legal protection of their health and well-being (112). Internationally, medical associations are developing programmes to promote the role of medical ethics in the protection of human rights (113) and to educate their members in the role of medical ethics in practice and research (114, 115). Such initiatives are praiseworthy but sporadic.

The need for vigorous and sustained scrutiny of women's health status is considerable at national, regional and international levels. Effort for advancement requires resources of many types. These include education of health professionals in human rights law and education of human rights advocates in how to acquire and interpret health data and extract the elements that are legally significant. Health professionals and human rights advocates, inspired by the goal of promoting and protecting women's health, should inform advocacy with health data by employing their knowledge of prevailing and achievable practices and the goals of international human rights treaties.

The above proposals would receive a powerful stimulus in the development and effective implementation of the principles for the promotion and protection of women's health referred to in Chapter 4. These principles would particularly address health status factors, health service factors and conditions affecting the health and well-being of women. On the basis of such principles, efforts could be made towards the development of specific guidelines for the legal promotion and protection of women's health.

With evidence of practice and advocacy of principle, appropriate mechanisms at all levels can determine standards of observance of women's rights to health that will identify injustice and illuminate the path to reform.

Notes and references

1. Constitution of the World Health Organization. In: *Basic Documents*, 39th ed. Geneva, World Health Organization, 1992.

2. The United Nations Charter, 1945.

3. Universal Declaration of Human Rights. In: *Human rights - a compilation of international documents*. Geneva, United Nations, 1993: 1.

4. International Covenant on Civil and Political Rights. In: *Human rights - a compilation of international documents*. Geneva, United Nations, 1993: 20.

5. International Covenant on Economic, Social and Cultural Rights. In: *Human rights - a compilation of international documents*. Geneva, United Nations, 1993: 8.

6. *European Convention for the Protection of Human Rights and Fundamental Freedoms.* New York, United Nations, 1959: 221 (United Nations Treaty Series 13).

7. European Social Charter, adopted 18 October 1961. *Human rights in international law: basic texts.* Strasbourg, Council of Europe Press, 1992.

8. *American Convention on Human Rights.* Washington, Organization of American States, 1969: 1 (Organization of American States Treaty Series).

9. *African Charter on Human and Peoples' Rights.* Organization of African Unity, 1981 (Document CAB/Leg/67/3/Rev.5).

10. International Convention on the Elimination of All Forms of Racial Discrimination. In: *Human rights - a compilation of international documents*. Geneva, United Nations, 1993: 66.

11. Convention on the Rights of the Child. United Nations General Assembly Resolution 44/25. 44. United Nations General Assembly Official Resolutions Supplement 49, 1989 (United Nations document A/44/736).

12. Convention Against Torture and Other Cruel, Inhuman or Degrading Treatment or Punishment. In: *Human rights - a compilation of international documents*. Geneva, United Nations, 1993: 293.

13. Convention relating to the Status of Refugees. In: *Human rights - a compilation of international documents*. Geneva, United Nations, 1993: 634.

14. Convention on the Elimination of All Forms of Discrimination against Women. In: *Human rights - a compilation of international documents*. Geneva, United Nations, 1993: 150.

15. *Health dimensions of economic reform*. Geneva, World Health Organization, 1992.

16. *The girl child: an investment in the future*. New York, UNICEF, 1990.

17. Koblinsky M, Timyan J, Gay J. *The health of women: a global perspective*. Boulder, CO, Westview Press, 1993.

18. *Women's health: across age and frontier*. Geneva, World Health Organization, 1992.

19. Dan AJ, Lewis LL. *Menstrual health in women's lives*. Chicago, University of Illinois Press, 1992.

20. Sherwin S. *No longer patient: feminist ethics and health care*. Philadelphia, Temple University Press, 1992.

21. Williams G. *The sanctity of life and the criminal law*. New York, Faber, 1958.

22. Cook RJ. Human rights and infant survival: a case for priorities. *Columbia human rights law review*, 1987, 18:1-41.

23. United Nations Commission on Human Rights. Resolution 1993/22 on the Right to Development (United Nations document E/CN.4/1993/L.11/Add.4).

24. Himes JR. Reflections on indicators concerning the rights of the child: the development and human rights communities should get their acts together. *Background paper for the Seminar on Appropriate Indicators to Measure Achievements in the Progressive Realization of Economic, Social and Cultural Rights, Geneva, January 1993* (United Nations document HR/Geneva/1993/Sem/BP.26).

25. Hamilton JA. Guidelines for avoiding methodological and policy-making biases in gender-related health research in public health service. In: *Women's health: report of the public health task force on women's health issues*. Washington, DC, Department of Health and Human Services, 1985.

26. American Medical Association Council on Ethical and Judicial Affairs. Gender disparities in clinical decision making. *Journal of the American Medical Association*, 1990, 266: 559-562.

27. *Women, health and development: progress report by the Director-General*. Geneva, World Health Organization, 1992 (unpublished document WHO/FHE/WHD/92.5, available from Division of Family Health, World Health Organization, 1211 Geneva 27, Switzerland).

28. Van Der Kwaak A. Female circumcision and gender identity: a questionable alliance? *Social science and medicine*, 1992, 35: 777-787.

29. A traditional practice that threatens health - female circumcision. *WHO chronicle*, 1986, 40: 31-36.

30. Ferguson A. Women's health in a marginal area of Kenya. *Social science and medicine*, 1986, 23(1): 23.

31. Fathalla MF. Reproductive health: a global overview. *Annals of the New York Academy of Sciences*, 1991, 626: 1-10.

32. Abou-Zahr C, Royston E. *Maternal mortality: a global factbook.* Geneva World Health Organization, 1991 (unpublished document WHO/MCH/MSM/91.3 available from Division of Family Health, World Health Organization, 1211 Geneva 27, Switzerland).

33. Maine D. *Safe motherhood programs: options and issues.* New York, Columbia University Center for Population and Family Health, 1991.

34. Safe Motherhood conference conclusions. *Lancet*, 1987, i: 670.

35. Royston E, Armstrong S, eds. *Preventing maternal deaths.* Geneva, World Health Organization, 1989.

36. Mitchell JL. Women, AIDS, and public policy. *AIDS and public policy journal*, 1988, 3(2): 50.

37. Mitchell JL et al. HIV and women: current controversies and clinical relevance. *Journal of women's health*, 1992, 1: 35-39.

38. Gollub EL, Stein ZA. Commentary: the new female condom - item 1 on a women's AIDS prevention agenda. *American journal of public health*, 1993, 83: 498-500.

39. Gillon R. Refusal to treat AIDS and HIV positive patients. *British medical journal*, 1987, 294: 1332-33.

40. Melica F. Fear of contracting HIV infection and ethical behaviour in medical care. In: Melica F, ed. *AIDS and human reproduction.* Basel, Karger, 1992.

41. Rosenberg ML, Stark E, Zahn MA. Interpersonal violence: homicide and spouse abuse. In: Last JM, ed. *Public health and preventive medicine*, 12th edition. Norwalk, CT, Appleton-Century-Crofts, l986: 1399-1426.

42. Vlassoff C, Bonilla E. Gender-related differences in the impact of tropical diseases on women: what do we know? *Journal of biosocial science*, 1994, 26: 37-53.

43. What doctors don't know about women: a special report. *The Washington Post*, 8 December 1992.

44. United Nations Development Programme. *Human development report 1992.* New York, Oxford University Press, 1992.

45. *Development of indicators for monitoring progress for health for all by the year 2000.* Geneva, World Health Organization, 1981 (Health for All Series No. 4).

46. *Implementation of the Global Strategy for Health for All by the Year 2000: second evaluation. Eighth report on the world health situation*. Geneva, World Health Organization, 1993.

47. Jabine T, Claude R, eds. *Human rights and statistics: getting the record straight*. Philadelphia, University of Pennsylvania Press, 1992.

48. *The Limburg Principles on the Implementation of the International Covenant on Economic, Social, and Cultural Rights* (United Nations document E/CN.4/1987/17). Annex published in *Human rights quarterly*, 1987, 9: 122-135.

49. Turk D. *The realization of economic, social and cultural rights* (United Nations document E/CN.4/Sub.2/1990/19).

50. Hauserman J. The use of indicators to measure realization of the right to take part in cultural life. *Background paper for the Seminar on Appropriate Indicators to Measure Achievements in the Progressive Realization of Economic, Social and Cultural Rights, Geneva, January 1993* (United Nations document HR/Geneva/1993/Sem/BP.28/Rev.1).

51. *Conclusions and Recommendations of the Seminar on Appropriate Indicators to Measure Achievements in the Progressive Realization of Economic, Social and Cultural Rights, Geneva, January 1993*. Geneva, United Nations (forthcoming).

52. WHO Resolution EB85.R5, 1990. *Handbook of resolutions and decisions of the World Health Assembly and the Executive Board*, volume III, 3rd ed. Geneva, World Health Organization, 1993.

53. Bartlett KT. Feminist legal methods. *Harvard legal review*, 1990, 103: 829-888.

54. Buergenthal T. To respect and to ensure: state obligations and permissible derogations In: Henkin L, ed. *The International Bill of Rights: The Covenant on Civil and Political Rights*. New York, Columbia University Press, 1981.

55. Alston P, Quinn G. The nature and scope of States Parties' obligations in the International Covenant on Economic, Social and Cultural Rights. *Human rights quarterly*, 1987, 9: 156-229.

56. *Salud para la mujer, mujer para la salud* (Health for women, women for health). Bogota, Ministry of Public Health, 1992.

57. Colombian Presidential Decree, No. 1398 of 3 July 1990.

58. Plata MI. Reproductive rights as human rights: the Colombian case. In: Cook RJ, ed. *Women's international human rights*. Philadelphia, University of Pennsylvania Press (forthcoming).

59. The Constitution of Colombia, 1991, article 42.

60. *Paulista Convention on the Elimination of All Forms of Discrimination against Women*. Minneapolis, International Women's Rights Action Watch, 1992.

61. *Report on the regional seminar on traditional practices affecting the health of women and children in Africa.* Geneva, Inter-African Committee on Traditional Practices Affecting the Health of Women and Children, 1987.

62. *Report of the Special Rapporteur: traditional practices affecting the health of women and children* (United Nations document E/CN.4/Sub.2/1991/6).

63. Judgement of 10 July 1987, Cour d'Appel, Case of Fofana Dala Traore (convicted of circumcising her daughter contrary to French law), reported in *Le Monde*, 13 July 1987.

64. *Annual review of law and population*, 1987: 205.

65. Cook RJ, Maine D. Spousal veto over family planning services. *American journal of public health*, 1987, 77: 339-344.

66. Sieghart P. *The international law of human rights.* Oxford, Oxford University Press, 1983.

67. United Nations document CCPR/C/21/rev.1 at para 5, 19 May 1989.

68. McLaurin K et al. Health systems role in abortion care: the need for a pro-active approach. *Issues in abortion care*, 1991, 1:34.

69. *Technical and managerial guidelines for abortion care.* Geneva, World Health Organization (in press).

70. Cook RJ. International protection of women's reproductive rights. *New York University journal of international law and politics*, 1992, 24: 647, 688-696.

71. Dickens BM. Reproduction law and medical consent. *University of Toronto law journal*, 1985, 35: 255-286.

72. Brazilian Code of Ethics, Chapter VI, Article 52, 1965. Cited in Merrick T: Fertility and family planning in Brazil. *International family planning perspectives*, 1983, 9: 110.

73. Barros FC et al. Epidemic of caesarean sections in Brazil. *Lancet*, 1991, 338: 167.

74. Giesen D. *International medical malpractice law.* Boston, Martinus Nijhoff, 1988.

75. Eriksson MK. *The Right to Marry and to Found a Family: a world-wide human right.* Uppsala, Justus Forlag, 1990.

76. United Nations document CCPR/C/21/Rev.1/Add.2, 19 September 1990.

77. For the origins of these rights, see *Population and human rights: proceedings of the Expert Group Meeting on Population and Human Rights, Geneva, 3-6 Apr 1989.* Geneva, United Nations, 1989.

78. *Results of the Twelfth Session of the Committee on the Elimination of Discrimination against Women, February 1993* (United Nations document E/CN.6/1993/CRP.2).

79. See also *Report on equality between women and men: the right to free choice of maternity.* Council of Europe, 1993 (Document 6781).

80. Colombian Ministry of Public Health, Resolution 1531 of 6 March 1992.

81. Wasserheit J. The significance and scope of reproductive tract infections among third world women. *International journal of gynaecology and obstetrics,* 1989, 3: 145-168.

82. Germain A et al., eds. *Reproductive tract infections: global impact and priorities for women's reproductive health.* New York, Plenum Press, 1992.

83. *Reproductive tract infections in women in the third world.* New York, International Women's Health Coalition, 1991.

84. *Bruggeman and Scheuten v. Federal Republic of Germany,* 3 Eur. H.R. 244, 1977.

85. *Paton v. United Kingdom,* App. No. S416/78, 3 Eur. H.R. Rep. 408, 1980.

86. *Open Door Counselling Ltd and Dublin Well Women Centre Ltd v. Ireland,* 14 Eur. H.R. Rep. 131, 1992, 15 Eur. H.R. Rep. 244, 1993.

87. *Kjeldsen, Busk Madsen and Pedersen v. Denmark,* 1 Eur. H. R. Rep. 711, 1976.

88. Byrnes A. CEDAW's Tenth Session. *Netherlands quarterly of human rights,* 1991, 3: 332-358.

89. *World health statistics annual.* Geneva, World Health Organization, 1988: viii.

90. *International digest of health legislation,* 1992, 43(2): 413-423.

91. *Status of women and family planning.* New York, United Nations, 1975 (United Nations document E/CN.6/575/Rev.1).

92. Sai F, Nassim J. The need for a reproductive health approach. *International journal of gynaecology and obstetrics,* 1989, 3: 103-114.

93. *Better health through family planning. Recommendations of the International Conference on Better Health for Women and Children through Family Planning, Nairobi, Kenya, October 1987.* London, International Planned Parenthood Federation, 1987.

94. Council of Europe Report Series, Note 112.

95. Cook RJ. Abortion laws and policies: challenges and opportunities. *International journal of gynaecology and obstetrics,* 1989, 3: 61-87.

96. Knoppers BM. Abortion law in francophone countries. *American journal of comparative law,* 1990, 38: 889.

97. *Abortion policies: a global review* (United Nations document: ST/ESA/SERA/129).

98. Henshaw S. Induced abortion: a world view. *Family planning perspectives*, 1990, 22: 76-89.

99. *Creating common ground: women's perspectives on the selection and introduction of fertility regulation technologies.* Geneva, World Health Organization, 1991 (unpublished document WHO/HRP/ITT/91, available from Special Programme of Research, Development and Research Training in Human Reproduction, World Health Organization, 1211 Geneva 27, Switzerland).

100. *Towards a women's health research agenda: findings of the scientific advisory meeting.* Washington, DC, Society for the Advancement of Women's Health Research, 1991.

101. *The National Institutes of Health Guide, 1990*, 19(31): 18.

102. Boland R. RU 486 in France and England: corporate ethics and compulsory licensing. *Law, medicine and health care*, 1992, 20: 226-234.

103. Code de Commerce, Brevets d'Invention, articles 37-40, 2 January, 1968.

104. Declaration on the Elimination of Violence against Women, adopted by the United Nations General Assembly, 20 December 1993 (Resolution 48-104).

105. Hannum H. *Guide to international human rights practice.* Philadelphia, University of Pennsylvania Press, 1992.

106. An-Na'im A. Human rights in the Muslim world: socio-political conditions and scriptural imperatives. *Harvard human rights journal*, 1990, 3: 13-52.

107. *Women's rights, human rights: Asia Pacific reflections.* Kuala Lumpur, Asia Pacific Forum on Women, Law and Development, 1993.

108. Buquicchio-de Boer. *Sexual equality in the European Convention on Human Rights.* Strasbourg, Council of Europe, 1989 (Document EG/89/3/1989).

109. Beyani C. Toward a more effective guarantee of the enjoyment of human rights by women in the inter-American system. In: Cook RJ, ed. *The human rights of women: national and international perspectives.* Philadelphia, University of Pennsylvania Press (forthcoming).

110. Medina C. Women's rights as human rights: Latin American countries and the Organization of American States. In: Diaz-Diocaretz and Zavala, eds. *Women, feminist identity and society in the 1980s, selected papers.* Amsterdam, John Benjamin Publishing Co., 1985.

111. Weston B et al. Regional human rights regimes: a comparison and appraisal. *Vanderbilt journal of transnational law*, 1987, 20: 585, 589-590.

112. Plata MI. Family law and family planning in Colombia. *International family planning perspectives*, 1988, 14: 109-111.

113. *Report of workshop on the role of medical ethics in the protection of human rights.* London, Commonwealth Medical Association, 1993.

114. See, for example, *International guidelines for biomedical research involving human subjects.* Geneva, Council for International Organizations of Medical Sciences, 1993.

115. Sureau C. Activities of the Committee for the Study of Ethical Aspects of Human Reproduction. *International journal of gynaecology and obstetrics,* 1989, 28: 299-307.

ANNEX 1

States Parties to the Convention on the Elimination of All Forms of Discrimination against Women (as at 1 January 1994)

Angola, Antigua and Barbuda, Argentina, Australia, Austria, Bahamas, Bangladesh, Barbados, Belarus, Belgium, Belize, Benin, Bhutan, Bolivia, Bosnia and Herzegovina, Brazil, Bulgaria, Burkina Faso, Burundi, Cambodia, Canada, Cape Verde, Central African Republic, Chile, China, Colombia, Congo, Costa Rica, Croatia, Cuba, Cyprus, Czech Republic, Denmark, Dominica, Dominican Republic, Ecuador, Egypt, El Salvador, Equatorial Guinea, Estonia, Ethiopia, Finland, France, Gabon, Gambia, Germany, Ghana, Greece, Grenada, Guatemala, Guinea, Guinea-Bissau, Guyana, Haiti, Honduras, Hungary, Iceland, India, Indonesia, Iraq, Ireland, Israel, Italy, Jamaica, Japan, Jordan, Kenya, Lao People's Democratic Republic, Latvia, Liberia, Libyan Arab Jamahiriya, Lithuania, Luxembourg, Madagascar, Malawi, Maldives, Mali, Malta, Mauritius, Mexico, Mongolia, Morocco, Namibia, Nepal, Netherlands, New Zealand, Nicaragua, Nigeria, Norway, Panama, Paraguay, Peru, Philippines, Poland, Portugal, Republic of Korea, Romania, Russian Federation, Rwanda, Saint Kitts and Nevis, Saint Lucia, Saint Vincent and the Grenadines, Samoa, Senegal, Seychelles, Sierra Leone, Slovakia, Slovenia, Spain, Sri Lanka, Suriname, Sweden, Tajikistan, Thailand, Togo, Trinidad and Tobago, Tunisia, Turkey, Uganda, Ukraine, United Kingdom of Great Britain and Northern Ireland, United Republic of Tanzania, Uruguay, Venezuela, Viet Nam, Yemen, Yugoslavia, Zaire, Zambia, Zimbabwe

Human rights applicable to women's health

	Universal Declaration of Human Rights	Int'l Covenant on Civil & Political Rights	Int'l Covenant on Economic, Social & Cultural Rights	Convention on the Elimination of all Forms of Discrimination against Women	Convention on the Rights of the Child	European Convention on Human Rights and its 5 Protocols & Social Charter	American Convention on Human Rights and Its Protocol	African Charter on Human & Peoples' Rights
Right of women to be free from all forms of discrimination	1, 2	2(1), 3, 4	2(2), 3	1, 2, 4	2	14	1	2, 18(3) 28 (duty)
Right to political participation	21	25	–	7, 8	–	10, 11, 14	16, 23	13
Right to information, opinion & expression	19	19	–	10(e), 14(b), 16 (e)	12, 13, 17	10	13	9
Freedom of assembly & association	20	21, 22	8	–	15	11	15, 16	10, 11
Right to religion/ freedom of thought	18	18	–	–	14, 30	9	12, 13	8
Right to survival	3	6	–	–	6	2	4	4
Right to liberty & security	13	9	–	–	37(b)-(d)	5	7	6
Right to be free from torture/ill-treatment	5	7	–	–	19, 34, 37(a)	3	5	5
Right to marry and found a family	16	23	10	16	8, 9	12	17	18
Right to private and family life	12	17	10	16	16	8	11	4, 5
Right to education	26	–	13, 14	10, 14(d)	28,29	Protocol 1:2	26	17
Right to health and health care	25	–	12	11(f), 12, 14(b)	24	Charter: 11,13	26; Protocol 9,10	16
Right to benefits of scientific progress	27(2)	–	15(1)(b), 15(3)	–	–	–	26	22